RIZVI'S
RISK
MANAGEMENT
PROFESSIONAL
(PMI–RMP®)

EXAM PREP GUIDE

S. HASNAIN RIZVI

PMP, CBAP, PMI-ACP, PMI-RMP, PMI-SP, CSM, CISA, CISM, CRISC, CSSGB,
CPCU, CITP(FELLOW), CDIA+, PROJECT+, OPM3 CERTIFIED CONSULTANT, PHD

To the Almighty, for giving me the strength
and opportunity to experience life;

To those Leaders whose sacrifices and contribution
have nurtured humankind's advancement;

To my family, with love and thanks
for their unwavering support.

ACKNOWLEDGMENTS

"In learning you will teach, and in teaching
you will learn."

PHIL COLLINS

There are many people to thank who have influenced this book. Most notably, it is the more than 15,000 students who have given me an opportunity to facilitate their professional development over the years.

I also wish to acknowledge those leaders and project managers who have inspired me during my professional career. They include Mario Stagliano, Amanda Coones, Peter Marsiglia, Salim Walji, Fred Hunt, Kari Van Gundy, Monica Bennett, Christine Locksy, Alisa Ahlstone-Lewis, Rick Healey, Lori-Ann Companion, Randy Rein, CJ Knapp, Yung Wu, Holly Zax, Cica Mijatovic, Garrett Carmody, David Epand, Willy Tang, and Raymond Deschamps.

I am also in debt to the many associates and business partners whom I have worked with over the years. You all have made my life richer.

I wish to thank Ms. M.A. Kazmi for providing constructive feedback to improve this final product.

My final note of gratitude goes out to a leader extraordinaire— my father. I have asked a great deal of you over the years, and you have always been there. To you and to all others who have helped me along life's journey, I am most grateful.

CONTENTS

TABLE OF FIGURES

INTRODUCTION
USING THIS STUDY GUIDE

Risk is inherent in all business practices, processes, and decisions. The rapid growth of global markets and prevailing economic uncertainty are making it increasingly necessary for organizations to become more proactive and responsive to risk in order to be successful. Yet many organizations today face a crisis in project risk management. The introduction of total quality management, continuous improvement programs, and the drive to radically redesign business processes require an alignment with strong project risk management skills. Proficiency in these skills is a prerequisite to managing change and growth at all levels. All stakeholders, including project managers, engineers, business analysts, and risk managers, stand to benefit by acquiring risk management expertise or hiring those that already have it.

A logical course of action for project leaders and associates is to seek out a structured and reputed certification by which unique expertise and competency in assessing and identifying project risks, mitigating threats, and capitalizing on opportunities are cultivated. The Project Management Institute's (PMI®) PMI Risk Management Professional (PMI-RMP®) credential benefits those specializing in the area of project risk management or those that would like to validate their experience and knowledge of this subject matter. Project risk management as a specialist field is expanding due to the increasing complexity and diversity of new technologies and the need for additional interrelated competencies.

To meet these challenges, this guide will help you pass the PMI-RMP® exam on your first attempt. Navigating the certification track will be manageable if you methodically follow this guide on your journey towards earning this in-demand credential.

Keep the end goal in mind. When you earn the PMI-RMP® credential, your organization will turn to you as their risk management specialist. You will become an essential member of your project team with the knowledge to actively assess, manage, and, where possible, eliminate risk. Having a solid grounding in project risk management and knowing how to use the tools and techniques in this guide are essential skills that will carry your career forward years into the future.

This easy-to-follow guide is going to prepare you to pass PMI's PMI-RMP® exam by helping you understand each of the specific steps involved in the project risk management processes. When you learn how to correctly use the tools and techniques to effectively work with risk in a variety of projects, passing the exam will no longer appear to be as daunting a goal.

This guide fully elaborates on the key principles and practices that you need to digest in project risk management along with exposing you to real-world scenarios to allow you to see how they work in different contexts. From gaining a solid understanding of the five key Domains of PMI-RMP® to testing your knowledge at the end of each section, this study guide will help you retain core information that will help you cross the finish line successfully.

Preparing for such a critical exam does not have to be a daunting process. Create a defined plan of action. All you need is to commit undivided attention to work through each chapter. You can test how well you have understood that information with the user-friendly "Study Success" area. There you will answer sample questions that emulate actual questions found in the PMI-RMP® exam.

I first ground you in the key elements of the theory of project risk management. The guide then helps you build on each day's knowledge by introducing you to new concepts and techniques. Through the use of this guide, you can go from being someone who lacks project risk management expertise to being a certified risk specialist who will be an asset to any project team.

Earning the PMI-RMP® credential may not be easy, but it is your challenge. Embrace it.

Success starts here.

CHAPTER 1

RIZVI'S PRINCIPLES OF SUCCESSFUL PROJECT MANAGEMENT

"Human beings, who are almost unique in having the ability to learn from the experience of others, are also regradeable for their apparent disinclination to do so."

DOUGLAS ADAMS

The goal of this book is to ensure that you pass the PMI-RMP® certification exam and do it with a full understanding of what it means to be in charge of project risk management. To begin, it is essential that we start with learning the core competencies needed to be a successful project management leader. We have been seduced by management catchwords like 'excellence', 'greatness,' 'transformation,' etc., but we have, in the process, somehow lost sight of the basics essential to managing projects. Certain critical must-haves should never be forgotten as you work towards your professional goals. I have developed RIZVI'S™ to capture these underlying competencies of project leadership and management.

R is for Respect

Strong project leadership begins with the trust that you form with your team members, which can only be established through respect. Project managers must treat their associates with the utmost respect.

Not only does that get each person in the team fully invested in the project but it automatically engenders respect for you in their eyes.

The only effective method in this "give-and-take" process of gaining respect is to model ideal behavior. Before knowledge, skills, and competency, your team will look to you to understand their own roles in the project team. Your behavior will mold how the team grows into the identified roles. As you define roles, treat your team with respect to promote an atmosphere of consideration, friendly and productive discussion, and collaboration.

The ideal behavior that you model should also include working on your time management skills and being conscious of your body language as well as actively listening to and collectively reaching decisions with valuable input from your team. Emphasize the need for honesty and transparency at all times, and get the technical elements right. But above all, never stop revisiting past processes with the goal of continuous improvement.

Be polite and considerate. Effective project management requires project leaders to control their tempers and at times deal with issues in private rather than berating team members in front of colleagues. This preserves the individual's self-esteem and, in turn, his or her confidence and productivity. By considering the opinions, ideas, and efforts of your team, you will earn their trust and respect[1]—which will ensure the success of every project.

As you step into the demanding role of a project manager, you cannot allow ego or excessive control to impede your leadership style. This includes avoiding micromanagement of your staff. Not only does that take time from your core responsibilities but it may also lead to your team's losing faith in you because it indicates that you lack confidence in their capabilities. Grant your team members the space they need to evolve into top notch contributors. Combine this with lessons-learned sessions and retrospectives. Constructive coaching at both the team and the individual level is most effective in reducing risks associated with the lack of effective social dynamics of a team.

---

1   Brad Egeland, Earning Respect as a Project Manager by Delivering Consistently, http://blog.entry.com/earn-project-management-respect

This is how respect is won. A project manager that is not respected is not trusted[2]—which causes dysfunction and disorder in the team. Lead, work, and inspire by example.

I is for Integrity

It is essential for the modern project manager to value and emanate integrity. If you are consistently honest and remain true to your responsibilities, people will perceive you as an honest person. Once you have developed credibility, whatever you say will be valued and considered to be the truth; your team will follow you when you give directions, and your clients or supervisors will trust you when you make a commitment. You will avoid a mismatch of expectations on all fronts and accomplish your project goals because there will be no discrepancies from the start.

A project manager with integrity will be honest with their team. Expectations will be clearly outlined, and the intentions, opinions, and quality of work produced will be spoken about frankly and in the correct context to drive improvement on multiple levels.

It becomes your job to make sure that a project is successful, which means being the driving force[3] behind your budget constraints, time limitations, and the scope that you have been given. In order to achieve this goal, each member of your team needs to be aware and on your side, and they need to know what their role in the project is at a micro level.

Your plan of action will result in shared success, so your team needs to believe in you. You must be able to get the job

---

2   Jonathan Feldman, Project Management Is Finally Getting Real Respect, http://www.informationweek.com/team-building-and-staffing/project-management-is-finally-getting-real-respect/d/d-id/1093342?

3   Integrity in Project Management, http://kellycrew.wordpress.com/2010/10/25/integrity-in-project-management/

done and do it in a manner that makes everyone feel invested in the hard work and achievement of the key goals. This means that integrity needs to become your primary goal. When you act with integrity, your team will be transformed into the best that it can be.

Truth has become a rare commodity in business, but it is a powerful asset since it motivates people and draws them closer to you. To become the kind of project manager who is seen as someone with integrity, work on your behavior. That means defining the actions that you are going to take then sticking to them—being accountable, consistent, and measuring the outcomes.

When a project manager has integrity, he or she is consistently reliable, and their methods, measures and techniques[4] are used because they have been proven to work. This means that you must be honest and open about all results, so that you can spot areas of improvement and actively work on them during a project.

Cultivate your integrity by always being on time and being true to your word. If you make a commitment, follow through on it. Leaders cannot be trusted if they are not predictable. An ethical anchor is key to keeping projects grounded in reality. Always accept responsibility for your failures, and do not pass the buck on to your team.

Ultimately, a good project manager is in charge of their team. This means that if your team fails, you have failed them. Remember to become the kind of project manager who reports accurately on what transpires so that no dishonesty creeps into your team dynamics.

A project manager is granted authority, but it takes their having a sensitive yet reliable plan of action for them to be

---

4   Project Management Integrity – At Least Try to Fake It, http://www. agilistapm.com/project-management-integrity-at-least-try-to-fake-it/

considered a leader with integrity. If done right, this becomes a huge asset for you, and it should be nurtured across the team so that you can effectively communicate and guide your team to success. Be impartial, be thorough, and always keep your eyes on the goal.

Z is for Zeal

A project leader's challenge is to inspire their team by sharing their zeal for delivering value. When a team has great energy and enthusiasm for the plan of action they are implementing, they have a much better chance of achieving goals that may sometimes appear to be unattainable. It is your job to work towards achieving key project goals. Wholehearted passion towards team objectives and team well-being is a vital tool for project managers to steer the team in the right direction.

Have you ever been to a meeting where the project manager or leader showed up late, talked about last night's game for ten minutes, and then finally got around to a brief summary of the project that you all have to work on? They spend most of the meeting on their phones or laptops, and then they leave early.

This is an extremely discouraging (and common) meeting format for many leaders. Teams perform better when they are motivated to do so—and this will come from you. The zeal that you learn to nurture will spark a fire in your team that results in greater successes. Imagine attending a meeting where the leader shows up early, is excited about their plan for the project, and works to share this excitement with their team. It is a far more effective approach.

Evidence[5] even suggests that when you select team members for your project and only consider their functional skills, it adds

---

5   Gary Hamilton, Gareth Byatt, Jeff Hodgekinson, Work Passion and Heart as Critical Behaviors: What Every Project Manager Should Bear in Mind, https://pmicie.org/images/downloads/Articles/9_general_article_work_passion_final.pdf

risk to the project. Choosing team members because they are passionate about the work mitigates risk. In the same way, the more passionate you are, the less risk you bring to each project you launch.

Ultimately, you add value to your team by being the driving force behind every plan that you all create and implement together. Plans work best when the team members involved are genuinely passionate and care about the intended outcome. When no one cares about the end result, poor work follows. Lack of inspiration creates risk.

Zeal is also a critical competency because each year the global environment changes; new trends and patterns emerge, and technologies influence what can and cannot be done. If you do not nurture a real passion for your field, you will stop learning and fall behind the pack. When a project manager stops learning, it sends the wrong message to fellow team members.

You need a healthy consideration for the end goal combined with a strong understanding that your attitude is what drives your team forward. Improvement and excellence are always within reach if you are effectively able to inspire your team. Without zeal, you will not pay enough attention to how your team is performing, and your results will be limited.

V is for Vision

Zeal alone cannot keep a team motivated for long; a shared vision is another huge motivator of success in any project. As a project manager, it is your job to ensure that stakeholders have a clear image of the goals for the completed product and project. This means that you need to have a solid and compelling vision for your project in the first place. This is a step that many managers neglect, which usually happens when zeal is missing from the behavioral formula.

Inspire a common vision in your team. Because you are in charge of working towards a specific goal and dealing with various limitations and constraints along the way, the vision needs to project a realistic yet invigorating view of the future. This view needs to be something worthy of attainment as well as being attainable so that it inspires all stakeholders when it is shared.

Once an inspiring vision has been created, it needs to be communicated to the core project team along with other key stakeholders. In fact, periodically reiterating the vision is critical to successfully leading the project team. A shared and clear vision helps the team understand the working parts and their roles in ensuring project success, providing the fuel for their motivation. Further, contextualizing your project goals is going to take a powerful shared vision.

A true visionary balances the short-term risk and opportunities along with the long-term risks and opportunities. Sharing insights, steps, tricks, and techniques[6] with your team will help them realize the potential of even the most complex and difficult projects.

The wonderful thing is that when a clear vision has been created, shared, and then achieved, it becomes fulfilling for everyone involved. Decisions become easier to make because everyone is on the same page, and insignificant obstacles become easier to sidestep because, with a shared vision, communication is always fluid as everyone works toward the common project objectives.

A very well-known principle states that you should "begin with the end in mind." Goal motivation is virtually useless if your team and you cannot imagine the outcome in the real

---

6   Lynda Bourne, Leadership: The Mission Is Vision, http://blogs.pmi.org/blog/voices_on_project_management/2013/04/leadership-the-mission-is-visi.html

world. The more you focus on that outcome, the more likely you are to achieve it.

Of course, during any project, obstacles will arise. These "fires" can only be extinguished effectively if a project manager keeps the team focused on the right objectives. It is so easy to become derailed when issues arise or to lose that excitement about a challenging goal. Many managers will change the goal to make it easier, losing out on the opportunity to do something really impressive.

Do not allow risks alone to determine your outcomes. It is the way that you deal with risk[7] that will ultimately either assist in your success or derail your progress towards that success. Stay grounded, and stick to your vision. Real vision takes motivation, sacrifice, and the belief that despite challenges, anything is possible if you have a plan.

I is for Innovation

An innovative approach to project management does more than help inspiring project managers achieve their goals. It also helps them develop their team, streamline techniques, and facilitate constant methodical improvement in such a way that challenges are dealt with and successes are achieved.

Innovation is a core competency for project managers because the field of project management is such an evolving niche. Every year, new techniques, technologies, methods, and processes are created that can rapidly improve the way that you handle your team, your projects, your budget, and your well-defined goals.

It is important that you make innovation a key concern in order to increase the quantity and quality of ideas and solutions

---

7   Brad Egeland, Project Management: Having Vision, http://pmtips.net/project-management-vision/

that your team develops. Innovation will keep you searching in the right direction when a problem needs to be solved. You will be able to find new ways to improve performance in many areas.

Your team will benefit as they discover new ways to collaborate, engage, and work together to achieve your vision objectives. As an essential part of any competent project management system, innovation is a way to evolve current systems so that they are able to continually improve—like many agile processes do.

By building innovation into your team culture, your team will constantly ask, "How can this be done better, faster, using less money or resources?" As a result, as time goes on, your team will become more efficient at problem solving on every level. This is important as project teams are instrumental in reducing risk in new projects.

Inspiring a culture of innovation[8] will also reveal who is genuinely passionate about their work and who needs more motivation. People who are inspired by what they do tend to be more innovative, while those who are simply going through the motions tend to stick to old processes and "tested" methods as they have no emotional investment in the goal.

Your team members need to be creative, outside-the-box thinkers so that you excel over time. Even if you begin on rocky ground, if you all work with your eyes on the prize and are determined to identify new solutions to old problems, positive things will happen. The more innovative you all become, the more creativity will drive your decisions.

This can become a habit that will be hugely beneficial to your team. If you are going to inspire innovation in your associates, you must also inspire creative thinking. Come

---

8   Global Dynamics of Innovations and Project Management, http://www.pmi.org/business-solutions/~/media/PDF/Business-Solutions/Global_innovations.ashx

up with interesting ways to look at an old problem. Host brainstorming sessions where everyone can contribute towards identifying potential solutions to an issue.

Innovation will make you a great project manager and allow your team to become accustomed to expecting change in each new project that they take on. This is a great practice and will keep people engaged, interested, and working towards success. Focus on how you will include innovation in your teams as a project manager. Status quo will prevail unless we learn to see our old project world with a new set of eyes.

S is for Solutions

A project manager's job description is complex and multifaceted. One of the most important elements of this role is to constantly look for better solutions within existing processes, methods, and systems. A solution-oriented mindset equips project managers with the ability to arrive at a better understanding of the challenges as well as potential areas for value-added improvement.

There is always room for refinement in how projects are managed. Whether it is developing your own skills and practical ability or developing the skills and abilities of your staff—to focusing on products, services, or results—there is always something that will benefit from your insight and assessment. Involve your team in identifying fresh approaches to problems.

Solutions for improved performance, time, resources, budgets, and project goals need to be managed as ongoing processes. If anyone on our team discovers a better method, it needs to be documented and tested. Projects company-wide can be improved if each team focuses on these assessments so that seeking continuous and improved solutions becomes common practice. A culture where progressive elaboration is embraced and valuable lessons learned are formally incorporated elevates the spirit of team members.

As you cultivate a culture of being solution-oriented, empower your associates with the philosophy of management by objectives (MBO). The defined end goal must be kept in mind. If necessary, frequently discuss what "done" looks like to ensure everyone is on the same page. You need to develop strategies for this, and strategies can always be improved—or customized—depending on the available resources. With each new project, fresh options to reduce or eliminate risk arise as well as the possibility of seeking out new opportunities.

But that means that you need to be a competent decision maker. As you move from one key decision to the next, take the time to mentor your team on how collaborative efforts are the fastest way to identify new methods of finding reliable solutions to problems.

As a project manager, you will frequently need to make key decisions regarding the project's people, processes, and product. A great project manager will always be on the lookout for new solutions. Goals[9] need to be measurable so that they can be achieved. There also needs to be consistent improvement in the achievement of these goals for you to be considered a solution-oriented project manager. Drive the goals, but do not forget to zero in on the steps required to make the next comparable project easier.

These are the core competencies for any great project manager in the modern age. To recap, the critical underlying competencies of project leadership and management are:

---

9   Project Management Checklist − Defining the Project Goal, http://wiki.en.it-processmaps.com/index.php/Project_Management_Checklist_-_Defining_the_Project_Goal

- **R** is for respect: A project manager needs to be a role model, not only for their own self-respect but to gain the respect of others. This respect will empower you to make changes.
- **I** is for integrity: The supreme quality of project leadership is integrity.
- **Z** is for zeal: You must inspire passion for unparalleled results from your team.
- **V** is for vision: A shared vision will keep your team united and on track.
- **I** is for innovation: Creative thinking leads to development and progress.
- **S** is for solutions: Keep the fire ignited for enthusiasm about continuous improvement as you build a solution-oriented culture.

Focus on RIZVI'S™ underlying competencies of project leadership and management to flourish as a project manager who delivers consistent and invaluable results.

CHAPTER 2

THE PMI-RMP® EXAM

"It seems that the necessary thing to do is not to fear mistakes, to plunge in, to do the best that one can, hoping to learn enough from blunders to correct them eventually."

ABRAHAM MASLOW

In order to sit for the PMI-RMP® exam, there are specific prerequisites one must fulfill. Examinees must be clear on the application requirements as well as the exam details. Along with outlining the prerequisites, this chapter will help clarify what format to expect on the day of the exam and where to concentrate your studies to increase your chances of passing the first time around. As you proceed through the material in subsequent chapters, retention should be your focus.

Preparing for the Exam

The PMI-RMP® designation reflects your level of expertise in the niche area of project risk management.

PMI has the following prerequisites for this certification:[10]

- A four-year degree (bachelors or the global equivalent) with at least 3,000 hours of project risk management experience and 30 hours of project risk management education.

OR

- A secondary diploma (high school or the global equivalent) with at least 4,500 hours of project risk management experience and 40 hours of project risk management education.

---

10   PMI-RMP Exam Guidance, http://www.pmi.org/en/Certification/PMI-Risk-Management-Professional-PMI-RMP/PMI-RMP-Exam-Prep.aspx

The PMI-RMP® exam is comprised of 170 multiple choice questions. PMI actively promotes studying for this exam with a guide or study aid because the subject is so diverse and complex. To adequately prepare for this exam, focus on getting the following details right:

- First, consult PMI's PMI-RMP® Handbook, where you will find details that include eligibility and steps to the application process.
- Review the current exam content outline to see a full breakdown of the test areas so that you know where to focus.
- Study the latest edition of *A Guide to the Project Management Body of Knowledge (The PMBOK® Guide)*. You should also pick up a copy of *PMI's Practice Standard for Project Risk Management*. Complimentary soft copies of these guides are available to PMI members. This exam prep guide complements PMI's guides and will help you navigate through your studies as you prepare for the exam.
- Read this guide sequentially through the chapters. Make the best use of your time, and fully absorb the information by dedicating a few hours to focused study each day. In order to ensure you retain the information, take an active and iterative approach to learning. You are more than likely going to need to read through the majority of this guide more than once. Re-read this guide as many times as needed to prepare for the test.

Application Process Outlined

In order to apply for the PMI-RMP® credential, follow these steps:

- Complete your PMI-RMP® application online at **www.pmi.org**. Keep in mind that once you begin your application, you have 90 days[11] to complete it online.

- Submit your application for review. PMI takes approximately five business days to review your application.

- Once your application has been approved, you will submit payment to take the test.

- After the payment is made, you may be notified that you have been selected for a random audit. If your application is selected for an audit, you will have 90 days to send in the requested supporting documentation. PMI's anticipated turnaround once the audit materials are received is approximately five business days. Once your eligibility is verified, you will be given the go-ahead.

- You have one year from the date of application approval to sit the exam. The exam can be taken up to three times within a 12-month period.

- Once you are certified, the PMI-RMP® credential must be maintained by earning 30 PDUs in the specific area of project risk management in every three-year cycle along with remitting the renewal fee. Credential holders can report their progress with PDUs via PMI's Continuous Certification Requirements (CCR) System.

This is all subject to your meeting the initial educational and work experience requirements. Without them, you will not be eligible to take the exam and earn the PMI-RMP® designation. The credential itself affirms your knowledge and experience in being able to assess and identify project risks and your ability to mitigate these threats while capitalizing on opportunities.

In essence, make sure that you cover the three essential components of eligibility for the PMI-RMP® exam, which

---

11   PMI-RMP Credential Handbook, http://www.pmi.org/Certification/~/media/ PDF/Certifications/pmi-RMP_handbook.ashx

include educational background, project risk management experience, and project risk management education. All experience must be accrued within the previous five years.

Exam Format

The proctored exam is 3 hours and 30 minutes. An extra 15 minutes of tutorial time is granted before the exam starts. Along with becoming familiar with the exam system, these 15 minutes can be used to conduct a major brain dump. The exam center will typically provide you with scratch paper and pencils. Anything you need to jot down can be done during this 15-minute time frame. These notes will come in handy when your energy starts to get drained as you progress through the somewhat strenuous exam.

The content for the exam is broken into five key areas as follows:

1. Risk Strategy Management makes up 19−20% of the exam.
2. Stakeholder Engagement constitutes 19−20% of the exam.
3. Risk Process Facilitation grabs a hefty 25−28% of the exam.
4. Risk Monitoring and Reporting accounts for 19−20% of the exam
5. Perform Specialized Risk Analyses comprises 14−16% of the test.

This adds up to 100% of your grade. When you study, focus on key definitions, important inputs and outputs, specific techniques, and key formulas.

The test includes 170 multiple choice questions. Only 150 questions are graded. Twenty questions are in "pre-release" mode, so they are not graded. Since the examinee does not know which are the beta questions, each question needs to be treated as the real deal.

One strategy to consider when taking the test is to skim over the questions and answer the ones that you are the most sure about. Then come back and spend the remainder of your time on questions that you have to give more thought to. You are also able to mark the questions that you want to review later on during the exam. You will be provided with a basic calculator during the exam.

The feedback I have received from the over 15,000 students I have trained in certification tracks globally is to split the exam into spurts with a quick break in between to revive your energy. For example, your strategy might be to tackle 50 questions and then take a quick, three-minute break. Keep in mind that the clock is still running during your break.

Dress in layers so you can adjust your comfort level based on the temperature in the exam hall.

While PMI has not announced an official exam passing grade, most experts assume it to be in the range of 70%. Play it safe and aim for a minimum grade of 75%. Practice tests can help you consistently achieve a grade above 75% to ensure that you are well prepared.

You will be notified of your score as soon as you complete the exam. Your scorecard will reflect your proficiency level by Domain. These correspond with the five Domains that are covered in the PMI-RMP® Exam Content Outline.

Exam Objectives

1. Risk Strategy and Planning

Your exam objectives are to achieve a high score in each section, so it makes sense to fully understand what each of these sections entail. The first Domain that you will focus on is called Risk Strategy and Planning, which accounts for 20% of the exam questions.

In this section,[12] you will be expected to look at activities related to the development of policies, processes, and procedures for risk assessment, planning, and responses. In this area, there are five tasks to consider:

1. Development of processes and tools that can calculate the risks for your stakeholders so that you can effectively assess and determine what your risk thresholds are for the project. The goal is to determine risk levels based on defined criteria.

2. Updating risk policies and procedures using reliable information, such as lessons learned from past projects and outputs of risk audits, to improve management effectiveness.

3. Developing and recommending generic project risk strategies that are based on your project objectives in order to establish an outline for your risk management plan.

4. Producing a risk management plan for your project on the basis of the following key inputs:
   ♦ Enterprise environmental factors
   ♦ Project management plan
   ♦ Stakeholder register
   ♦ Project charter
   ♦ Organizational process assets

5. Establishing evaluation criteria for risk management processes, based on project baselines and objectives, in order to measure the extent of project risks.

---

12   PMI Risk Management Professional, Exam Content Outline, http://www.pmi.org/~/media/Files/PDF/Certification/PMI-RMP%20Exam%20Content%20Outline_Final.ashx

You will need to focus on continuous process improvement as it applies to risk management as well as gain a solid understanding of management techniques for organizing and assessing project risk information.

This entails understanding metrics for measuring effectiveness in the project risk process and knowing about risk attitude concepts and risk breakdown structures as well as risk tolerance concepts. Once you have a grasp of this, you can proceed to the barriers to effective risk management and what project inputs, outputs, tools, and techniques look like in typical situations.

Finally, you will need to know about project risk contingencies and management reserves. You should understand how research and analysis techniques work. Risk strategy development methods, including the ability to assess stakeholder risk tolerance to build a consensus among them, will help you pass this initial section of the exam.

If you can distill your knowledge and focus on these five areas within the first Domain of risk strategy and planning, you will not only secure 20% of your overall grade but also will get the most out of your strategy and planning skills in project management.

2. Stakeholder Engagement

The second domain falls under Stakeholder Engagement, which accounts for 20% of your grade. Stakeholder engagement refers to activities that promote understanding project risk management for stakeholders and team members. You must understand risk tolerance, prioritizing project risk, and promotion of risk ownership to succeed here.

For these grades, you have to work through nine task areas. Task 1 helps you understand the value of risk management using interpersonal skills to attain shared accountability, responsibility, and ownership. Tasks 2 and 3 are about educating stakeholders in risk principles and processes to foster engagement and to help them implement these risk processes to ensure their constant application.

Tasks 4 and 5 center around the assessment of stakeholder risk using interviews and reviewing behaviors to establish project thresholds and identification of stakeholder risk attitudes and biases using analysis techniques to manage expectations and responses during a project lifecycle.

Tasks 6 and 7 involve engaging these stakeholders in a risk prioritization process based on tolerance and other criteria to optimize consensus and priorities and providing risk-related recommendations concerning risk strategy and planning, risk process facilitation, risk reporting, and specialized risk tasks via effective communication techniques to support risk-based decision making.

For tasks 8 and 9, you will focus on promoting risk ownership by communicating roles and responsibilities and engaging team members in developing risk responses to improve execution and meeting with other project stakeholders to share risk performance information so that everyone is aware of the implications of their projects.

3. Risk Process Facilitation

Risk Process Facilitation is concerned with activities that facilitate risk identification, evaluation, prioritization, and response among your team and will account for 25–28% of your grade. There are seven tasks to focus on in this section. Tasks 1 and 2 are about applying risk assessment processes and tools to quantify stakeholder risk tolerances and determine risk levels while facilitating identification using techniques that team members can understand.

Tasks 3 and 4 focus on facilitating the team's evaluation of identified risk using qualitative and quantitative tools to prioritize risk response planning and to facilitate the development of aligned risk response strategies and related actions to determine timely defined actions.

Tasks 5 and 6 are about facilitating the formulation of project contingency reserve based on risk exposure in the project to have resources to respond to realized risk and to provide risk data to analysts so that project risk is accurately reflected in cost and schedule estimates.

Last but not least, task 7 uses scenarios to validate potential risk responses and to evaluate key dependencies and requirements to enhance your project success. A great deal of knowledge is required to correctly answer these questions and pass the exam.

4. Risk Monitoring and Reporting

The fourth Domain involves Risk Monitoring and Reporting, which comprises seven tasks and accounts for up to 20% of your exam grade. Risk monitoring and reporting is concerned with activities relating to monitoring risk, evaluating risk response against established metrics, and communicating this performance to stakeholders and project teams.

The first and second tasks focus on documenting and updating project risk information using standard tools and techniques in order to maintain a current repository of project risk information and to coordinate with project managers using communication to integrate risk management in the project.

Tasks 3 and 4 pertain to the creation of periodic standard and custom reports using risk-related metrics as outlined in risk management plans to communicate risk management activities and statuses and to monitor risk response metrics by analyzing performance information, presenting it to stakeholders to ensure resolution of risk, and developing more response strategies to address additional risks.

Tasks 5 and 6 focus on analyzing risk process performance against established metrics to drive risk process improvements and to update your project risk management plan using the right internal and external inputs to keep the plan current and working. Task 7 captures risk lessons learned via a review of the plan, risk register, audits, and risk process performance reports and incorporates them into future risk planning.

5. Performing Specialized Risk Analyses

The final Domain section concerns performing Specialized Risk Analyses that focus on activities related to specialized quantitative and qualitative tools and techniques used by project risk management professionals. This accounts for 14−16% of your grade.

There are three tasks in this section, the first centered around evaluating the attributes of identified risk using advanced quantitative tools and qualitative techniques to estimate overall risk exposure of the project. The second task requires analyzing risk data produced during the project using statistical analyses and expert judgment to determine strengths and weaknesses in risk strategy and to recommend process improvements where necessary.

The third task involves performing specialized risk analysis using advanced tools and techniques to support stakeholder decision making for the project. You will need to be well versed in a number of areas, including advanced risk identification using tools for spotting threats and opportunities.

That means focusing on many complex areas of analyses and becoming adept at using specific tools to analyze and predict overall project risk. For all of these Domains, you will need to understand project risk management processes, frameworks, and theory and how these are utilized in real world scenarios.

Along with these skills, you should work on your understanding of risk principles, communication tools, models and channels, and leadership theory as it relates to this niche. This guide will help you work through the main areas so that you can understand what project risk management is all about and pass your test the first time.

CHAPTER 3

RISK MANAGEMENT FUNDAMENTALS

"People who don't take risks generally make about two big mistakes a year. People who do take risks generally make about two big mistakes a year."

PETER F. DRUCKER

There are six processes involved in project risk management, but before you can understand them, you need to start at the beginning. You already have a firm grasp of the core competencies that you should strive towards as a project manager; now you need to understand the fundamentals of risk management. That means looking at project management and your role as a project manager who is working towards reducing risk and increasing opportunities for your company. The first step is to correctly define project management.

What Is Project Management?

According to *The PMBOK Guide*, the skills of a successful project manager can be summarized into effective communications, budgeting, problem solving, team building, organizational capabilities, negotiation capacity, team leading, and influencing. These are the skills that produce project management excellence in the eyes of PMI.

The main difference between a project and operations is that projects are temporary, with a well-defined start and end date. These projects produce unique products, services, or results. Operations are seen as business as usual or an ongoing exercise that uses repetitive processes that produce the same result over and over again.

> Project management can be defined as the application of knowledge, skills, tools, and techniques to project activities to meet project requirements.[13]

The PMBOK Guide outlines five project management process groups that are mandatory in each project or project phase. These are initiating, planning, executing, monitoring and controlling, and closing.

1. *Initiating:* The processes that are performed to define new projects or a phase of an existing project by getting authorization to start those projects or phases; stakeholders are also identified during initiation.

2. *Planning:* The processes required to establish the scope of the project to refine the objectives and adequately define the course of action required to attain the objectives that the project is intended to achieve.

3. *Executing:* The processes that are performed to complete the work that was defined in the project management plan to satisfy project specifications and meet customer requirements.

4. *Monitoring and Controlling:* The processes that are needed to track, regulate, and review the progress and performance of your project, identify any areas where change is required, and initiate the relevant approved changes.

5. *Closing:* The processes performed to finalize all activities across all process groups to formally close the phase or project.

---

13   Project Management Body of Knowledge (PMBOK) Guide, http://www.itinfo.am/eng/project-management-body-of-knowledge-pmbok-guide/a

Figure 1: Project Management Process Groups

PMI defines each project lifecycle as including all five process groups. The same is true for the life cycle of a phase. A project is typically made up of several phases; the number of phases depends on the project's complexity.

In addition to risk management, there are nine other knowledge areas within project management. These are: integration management, scope management, time management, cost management, quality management, human resource management, communication management, procurement management, and stakeholder management.

What Is Project Risk Management?

Project risk management is one of the most important aspects of project management. According to PMI, risk management is one of the 10 key knowledge areas. Project risk is defined as "an uncertain event or condition that, if it occurs, has a positive or negative effect on a project's objectives."[14]

---

14   Project Risk Management, Wikipedia, http://en.wikipedia.org/wiki/Project_risk_management

Project risk management[15] involves many processes aimed at planning, identifying, analyzing, responding to and controlling a multitude of risk factors that may threaten the efficacy or end result of a specific project.

This makes project risk management an essential regular set of processes that must be integrated into all projects in the portfolio. Project risk management also focuses on impact to project goals and the ways in which risk can be managed to meet project objectives.

Project risk management not only deals with negative risks or threats but also positive risks or opportunities. By proactively identifying project risks, new opportunities are also discovered. Using risk management in a project can drastically change its outcomes for the better in a highly competitive business environment.

Project risk management is an integral component of effective organizational portfolio management. Non-value-added work needs to be reduced. Practices need to be streamlined, and risks must be identified early on so that potential pitfalls or mistakes can be prevented.

Simply communicating risks to your team members can have positive ramifications because it works towards empowering them to carry out tasks that can be improved, streamlined, and actively assessed according to their risk factors. With every project team member doing this, project outcomes can be rapidly improved across multiple levels.

When project risks are analyzed and opportunities are sought and undertaken, it lends itself to greater clarification of ownership. Assigning responsibility for specific tasks is one of the most important elements in ensuring that they are

---

15 Michael Stanleigh, Risk Management...The What, Why, and How, http://www.bia.ca/articles/rm-risk-management.htm

accomplished correctly for the benefit of key stakeholders. When people are held accountable as part of a risk management team, they are aware of the elements in their work that may disrupt or improve the eventual outcome.

When risk is analyzed and used to guide projects, it makes prioritization and planning much easier. With each project, new insights are collected, a process that benefits both subsequent iterations and phases in the current project as well as future projects as a valuable Organizational Process Asset. When risk responses are carefully planned out, it adds value to your project because the likelihood and impact of negative risks are reduced.

Project risk models and checklists can be built so that when similar projects are launched, it is immediately known what potential risks and rewards there may be. This facilitates accurate planning and strategy, and when all of these outcomes can be measured, it guarantees that resources, funding, and staff are not misappropriated for any reason.

A PMI Roadmap to Success

PMI is a leading global authority on project risk management. PMI offers more than eight different certifications to professionals in project, program, and portfolio management. PMI states that demand for skills in project management is on the rise, and where there is demand, there is a need for education.

PMI has disclosed that one-fifth of the world's GDP is spent on projects, amounting to just over $12 trillion[16] every year. Over 500,000 professionals have already been through the PMI certification process, choosing from one of their eight

---

16 What Are PMI Certifications?, http://www.pmi.org/Certification/What-are-PMI-Certifications.aspx

programs. This guide focuses on the PMI-RMP® certification.

The good news is that PMI gives you some of the tools you need to study and succeed in passing your exam. I recommend using both *The PMBOK Guide* and *The Practice Standard for Project Risk Management* when preparing for this exam. These two will cover the bodies of knowledge that you need to learn. This exam prep guide is a supplementary tool to be used in addition to the PMI resources. It breaks down and simplifies all of the core concepts and is a critical asset to successfully passing the exam.

Take advantage of PMI's online resources, especially the Knowledge Center. Different project lifecycles can influence project risk management. *The PMBOK Guide* covers the following types of project life cycles: predictive, iterative (incremental), and adaptive (agile). Risks can change the way that you plan and implement your projects—even how you communicate with your team.

This guide should be utilized to refresh your knowledge or to test specific sections of knowledge that you may struggle with. I will say this—what you put in is what you will get out. From learning about integration management to how to deal with risks as they relate to scope, time, cost, quality, and communications, you will be better off once risk management is a fundamental part of your project management approach.

Each chapter in this book should be carefully studied. When you are comfortable with the content, you should test yourself using the unique sample questions at the end of each chapter. If you score above 75% on each section, you are ready to move on to the next chapter.

Your Role in Project Risk Management

Project risk management and project management go hand in hand. You cannot run a successful project without fully understanding or preparing for the many risk–reward scenarios that may arise. If you do not, you may encounter serious obstacles and miss out on incredible opportunities.

One of the most important tasks that you will have as a project risk manager is to identify risks and determine how they might impede your project. Planning for these eventualities can help your team sidestep challenges and keep things moving forward according to the approved project plan—such as being on time and within budget.

As a project risk manager, it will be your job to assess risks on many levels. This means that at every stage of the project management process, you are looking at both the potential risks and the potential rewards through a very specific lens. Team selection, budget allocation, scheduling, and measuring of results are all key concerns.

Most importantly, it is your job to create a successful project risk management plan and strategy. This radically improves your chances of achieving your end goal—no matter how ambitious it may be.

The best part of being a project risk manager is that you can learn from the evidence. After several projects have been run, you will have a body of knowledge to work from. By measuring and analyzing risks in past projects, you can better plan for future obstacles. In fact, many project risk managers are using technologies to help them crunch the data so that people, processes, products, and services can be accurately analyzed.

Project risk managers impact all aspects of the project lifecycle. From the large elements like stakeholder engagement, budgeting, scheduling, quality control, and communication to the smaller elements of accurate process or model selection, you have a direct hand in shaping the success of your project. However, reaching a common consensus within your project team has always been a challenge. When you assess risk, this challenge is simplified as it helps you come to an agreement among your team members using data and evidence as warnings or attraction points.

Risk management begins before strategy is even considered. It is a method of determining which strategy or plan would be most viable based on current market conditions and past evidence. Best of all, project risk managers have the opportunity to improve the skills[17] of their team by teaching them about collaboration and consensus.

Moving forward, your tasks will include the following:

- Building risk management plans
- Identifying risk wherever it may be in your project
- Performing qualitative risk analysis
- Performing quantitative risk analysis
- Planning your risk responses
- Monitoring and controlling risks
- Communicating risks to your stakeholders and team members

Your behavior and the behavior of your team will determine how you approach risk, which means that your models will change depending on your team selections. The same can be said about the other elements of building a successful risk management plan.

---

17   Gary Hamilton, Risk Management and Project Management Go Hand in Hand, http://www.cio.com.au/article/385084/risk_management_project_management_go_hand_hand/

Project Risk Management Terminology

Here are some terms that you will need to know.

- **_Control Assessment_**: An assessment of the effectiveness of an existing control based on how it is operating
- **_Current Risk Rating_**: An estimated level of risk that takes existing controls into consideration
- **_Establishing Context_**: Defining internal and external parameters to be taken into account when managing risks and setting scope and criteria for the risk management policy
- **_Extreme Risks_**: Risks that requires immediate action
- **_Inherent Risk Rating_**: The level of risk without taking existing systems and procedures into account to control or manage risk
- **_Operational Risks_**: These relate to daily activities, operational business plans and objectives; they are short term and can impact many areas of business.
- **_Progressive Elaboration:_** A continuous iterative process of refining and further detailing the product characteristics based on more detailed information and insight that becomes available as the project progresses
- **_Project Risks_**: An uncertain event that, if it occurs, has a positive or negative effect on the prospects of achieving project objectives
- **_Residual Risk Rating_**: The remaining level of risk after all risk response plans have been implemented
- **_Risk_**: The effect of uncertainty on objectives
- **_Risk Acceptance_**: A risk response technique employed when the risk cannot be avoided or transferred or if the project team decides to accept the risk and its consequences. There are primarily two types of risk

acceptance strategies: passive acceptance and active acceptance. Passive acceptance requires no action beyond documenting the decision; active acceptance includes further action, such as setting aside a contingency to offset the effect of that risk.

- **Risk Analysis:** The process of comprehending the nature of risk to determine the level of risk posed
- **Risk Appetite:** The amount and type of risk that an organization is willing to pursue or retain
- **Risk Assessment:** Overall process of identifying risks using analysis and evaluation techniques
- **Risk Avoidance:** Informed decision not to be involved in an activity in order to avoid being exposed to a specific risk
- **Risk Management Process:** The systematic application of management procedures and practices involved in communicating; establishing the context for; and planning, identifying, analyzing, evaluating, treating, monitoring, and reviewing risks
- **Risk Matrix:** A tool for ranking and displaying risks by defining ranges for consequence and likelihood
- **Risk Tolerance:** An organization/stakeholders' readiness to bear the risk after risk treatment in order to achieve objectives
- **Risk Sharing:** A risk response technique for positive risks or opportunities that involves assigning partial or complete ownership of the risk to a third party that is in a better position to make sure the opportunity is realized

Performing Risk Activities: Things to Understand

There are dozens of elements involved in project risk management, and because all organizations are subject to risk, there is a perpetual threat that a crisis could result if a project manager fails to manage those risks properly. If you are unable to make a decision on what you should do, when to do it, or if you have done enough to achieve the objectives,[18] it means that you have not sufficiently looked at risks and made appropriate plans concerning those risks.

In order to effectively manage risks, you have to understand what it is. Your first priority is always to achieve your end goal; otherwise the project is pointless. The combination of decisions it will take for you to get this done depends on how much you understand about your team, your company, and the processes that you employ there.

Risk assessment typically contains three elements: First, you need to identify uncertain or vulnerable areas in your project plan then analyze the risks involved. Detail how these areas might impact the performance of your project as they relate to cost, duration, or team participation. Then prioritize these risks—know which ones to eliminate and which ones to manage or leave alone. Not all risks are bad; there are both positive and negative risks in projects.

According to *The PMBOK Guide*, a risk management plan is the way in which you define, monitor, and control risks throughout the project. It is created in the plan risk management process. The risk management plan does not define individual risk responses, but it does cover what level of risk (risk appetite) is tolerable, how risk will be managed, and who will be responsible for these risk activities.

It also delineates the cost and time to be allotted to risk activities and how well risk is communicated. This should include how risks are categorized, which can be done through the use of a risk breakdown structure.

---

18   Project Risk Management Principles, http://www.netcomuk.co.uk/~rtusler/project/principl.html

In addition, in the areas where you have identified potential risk in your project, you will need to plan for emergencies. Basic measure and control methods of tracking and analyzing each risk area can provide a great deal of information to help you make these decisions. If you can perform these risk activities on a basic level when you begin, eventually you will be able to handle far more complex and multifaceted projects.

Risk impacts scope, schedule, cost, performance, and quality in project management. Although it occurs in the future and is uncertain, it may have one or more causes and impacts. Usually a requirement, assumption, constraint, or condition creates the possibility of either a negative or positive outcome.

Understand that risk follows a set pattern of determination, but that it takes sound judgment to be a good project risk manager. It is the decisions that you make that will ultimately make you effective in your field. To place the project risk management process into context, here is a graphic outlining each essential stage.

PMBOK© PROJECT RISK MANAGEMENT OVERVIEW

PLAN RISK MANAGEMENT	IDENTITY RISK	PERFORM QUALITATIVE ANALYSIS
Inputs • Project management plan • Project charter • Stakehold register • Enterprise environmental factors • Organizational process assets **Tools & Techniques** • Analytical techniques • Expert judgment Meetings **Outputs** • Risk Management Plan	**Inputs** • Risk management plan • Cost management plan • Schedule management plan • Quality management plan • Human resource management plan • Scope baseline • Activity cost estimates • Activity duration estimates Stakeholder register • Project documents • Procurement documents • Enterprise environmental factors • Organizational process assets **Tools & Techniques** • Documentation reviews • Information gathering techniques • Checklist analysis • Assumptions analysis • Diagramming techniques • SWOT analysis • Expert judgment **Outputs** • Risk register	**Inputs** • Risk management plan • Scope baseline • Risk register • Enterprise environmental factors • Organizational process assets **Tools & Techniques** • Risk probability and impact assessment • Probability and impact matrix • Risk data quality assessment • Risk categorization • Risk urgency assessment • Expert judgment **Outputs** • Project documents updates

PMBOK© PROJECT RISK MANAGEMENT OVERVIEW

PERFORM QUALITATIVE ANALYSIS RISK	PLAN RISK RESPONSES	PERFORM QUALITATIVE ANALYSIS
Inputs	**Inputs**	**Inputs**
• Risk management plan	• Risk management plan	• Project management plan
• Cost management plan	• Risk register	• Risk register
• Schedule management plan	**Tools & Techniques**	• Work performance data
• Risk register	• Strategies for negative risks or threats	• Work performance reports
• Enterprise environmental factors	• Strategies for positive risks or opportunities	**Tools & Techniques**
• Organizational process assets	• Contingent response strategies	• Risk reassessment
	• Expert judgment	• Risk audits
Tools & Techniques		• Variance and trend analysis
• Data gathering and representation techniques	**Outputs**	• Technical performance measurement
• Quantitative risk analysis and modeling techniques	• Project management plan updates	• Reserve analysis Meetings
• Expert judgment	• Project documents updates	
		Outputs
Outputs		• Work performance information
• Project documents updates		• Change requests
		• Project management plan updates
		• Project documents updates
		• Organizational process assets updates

50

CHAPTER 4

WORKING WITH PLAN RISK MANAGEMENT

"First, have a definite, clear practical ideal; a goal, an objective. Second, have the necessary means to achieve your ends; wisdom, money, materials, and methods. Third, adjust all your means to that end."

ARISTOTLE

In the area of project risk management, PMI has developed a specific approach to deal with the challenges that arise with project risk. This five-step process is called "PIER-C."

- **P** stands for **Plan** Risk Management
- **I** stands for **Identify** Risks
- **E** stands for **Evaluate**: Performing both Qualitative and Quantitative Risk Analysis
- **R** stands for **Response**: Plan Risk Responses
- **C** stands for **Control** Risks

Every step will be defined at the beginning of each learning segment so that you can see how it fits in with the overall system. Make a mental note to learn these definitions as you will be tested on them!

What Is Plan Risk Management?

PIER-C: Plan Risk Management is the first process and neatly defines how risk management will be achieved through a specifically chosen method. The end goal of the first section is to have a fully developed risk management plan, which will describe in detail how your project's risk management process will function from start to finish.

Plan Risk Management is the first step taken in the Risk Management Process. When you, as the project risk manager, tailor your Risk Management Process and strategy to a specific project, it will be adapted to meet your stakeholder expectations and requirements.

Establishing these rules will help you govern and guide the eventual execution of all of your Project Risk Management processes. You need to know how your plan will integrate with your other project management processes so that they function effectively together.

Also, completing this process will help you to benchmark key areas and improve any future risk management activities.

A Risk Management Plan[19] is the document that you will prepare that will enable you to foresee risks, estimate impacts from this risk, and define responses to it that address the core problems in that risk. As the project progresses, a risk assessment matrix can be created as part of the risk management plan.

When risk is present in a project, it has the probability of occurring—and this could have either a positive or a negative impact on that project. Understanding risk and planning to identify, analyze, monitor, and control that risk are all part of your role as a project risk manager. To do this effectively, you need to know how to build a comprehensive risk management plan.

Plan risk management encompasses this process from beginning to end. The Risk Management Plan goes through progressive elaboration throughout the project lifecycle.

---

19   Risk Management Plan, https://www.phe.gov/about/amcg/toolkit/Documents/risk-management.pdf

The Plan Risk Management Process

The Plan Risk Management Process utilizes a model that focuses on a three-step approach to analysis. First, one needs certain inputs; tools and techniques are then used to ultimately generate the output of a risk management plan.

An input is defined in *The PMBOK Guide* as an item, whether internal or external to the project, that is required by a process before that process proceeds. For example, you bring certain inputs to a planning meeting and ensure that all team members understand how to transform these inputs into the key output of a risk management plan from this process.

Tools and techniques selection will impact your results and may require team training in their specific use. Outputs use these tools and techniques to produce the product that you want to have by the end of the meeting.

All 47 processes in *The PMBOK Guide*, including Plan Risk Management, consist of inputs, tools and techniques, and outputs. In this process, inputs include the project management plan, project charter, stakeholder register, enterprise environmental factors, and organizational process assets. Whatever your selection, a number of these inputs will be required to complete the Plan Risk Management process.

Once you have selected the inputs, your team will choose tools and techniques, which include analytical techniques, meetings, and expert judgment. These will facilitate delivering your output; namely, your complete Risk Management Plan.

This key document will provide the strategy with which risk management will be handled and approached throughout your project. The level of detail that you record will depend on the categories and levels of risks in your chosen project and the level of risk that your company is willing to take. The inner workings of this plan involve five key steps.

You will look at identifying risk, performing qualitative and quantitative analysis, planning your risk responses, and controlling your risks.

Project Risk Management in Practice!

James Townsend is a project risk manager working for a prominent up and coming tech start-up in Silicon Valley. He has been given a new project and has been told to work through the Plan Risk Management Process to formulate an effective Risk Management Plan.

James has his PMI-RMP® certification to help him prepare a plan that will significantly reduce the risk involved for his company in launching a new product into the market. He has put together a Risk team to assist in the creation of this plan.

After working out all of the details, James will have a complete and functional Risk Management Plan that can be used throughout the project lifecycle.

Follow James as he implements each step of the Plan Risk Management Process so that you can see how it is done in the real world and get prepared to answer questions on the PMI-RMP® exam.

Inputs Needed for Plan Risk Management

Once your team has been gathered, you will need to establish which inputs you want to bring to your meeting. A set of inputs is needed to eventually achieve the Plan Risk Management process. It is your job to get these five inputs in order.[20]

---

20   Risk Management Inputs, http://en.wikibooks.org/wiki/Project_Management/ PMBOK/Risk_Management#Inputs

- *Project Management Plan*: When planning risk management, all approved subsidiary management plans and baselines must be taken into account. The risk management is a critical component of the project management plan.
- *Project Charter*: The project charter provides formal approval for the project, so it is a source of formal and referent power to better manage project risks. The project charter also covers risks at a high level.
- *Stakeholder Register*: The stakeholder register outlines the roles of key stakeholders. This helps reduce conflicts.
- *Enterprise Environmental Factors*: This input is about risk attitudes and tolerances that are typically outside of the control of the project manager and risk manager. The degree of risk an organization is willing to tolerate will be inserted here. These factors can often include industry norms, processes, and procedures to be followed and issues such as laws and regulations that have a bearing on the nature of risk within a project.
- *Organizational Process Assets*: This input includes risk categories, definitions, templates, roles and responsibilities, and information on organizational risk tolerances. They are divided into categories, usually corporate knowledge, procedures, and processes. Templates and lessons learned from previous projects provide some useful learning opportunities here.

These inputs will help arm the team with the information necessary to spot risks in the new project and then manage them according to practices proven to be successful in the past. It will also help them discover new risks or new processes for managing those risks that will be more effective.

> ## Project Risk Management in Practice!
>
> James has spent some time reviewing old lessons learned from previous projects and has gathered the five necessary inputs to take to his meeting. These inputs are his project scope plan, a cost and schedule management plan, and a communications management plan. He has also brought data on enterprise environmental factors and organizational process assets to orient his team as they attempt to identify risks together.

Strategies, Tools and Techniques

At this early stage of planning, meetings are held by the project team to develop the risk management plan in collaboration with key stakeholders. This means that you, as the project risk manager, will need to host planning meetings with a team of selected participants and experts.

As a general rule, your chosen stakeholders should be invited to attend these planning meetings so that they can offer expert opinions and technical guidance. They will be the "Risk Team" and are either assigned to your project or you are given the opportunity to assemble a Risk Team of your own choosing.

The participants should include the following individuals:

- *The Project Risk Manager*: You fall into this role, also called the project manager in general terms.
- *Selected Team Members*: These are comprised of specially chosen or assigned team members who will help you assemble and execute your plan.
- *Key Stakeholders*: These are the people who stand the most to gain or lose if your project management plan succeeds or fails.

- ***Subject Matter Experts:*** Within any project, there will be subject matter experts that can add knowledge and shed light on specific issues.
- ***Stakeholders with Risk Responsibilities:*** These are stakeholders who have been assigned responsibilities within your Risk Team. They are directly involved in the process and should be proactively communicated with often.

This project team will meet to set out the basic plans for your Risk Management Process and will be responsible for managing the process as your project moves forward. That means being in charge of budgeting, schedule, assigning personnel responsibilities, and establishing risk templates.

Establishing risk templates involves customizing risk categories and definitions for ongoing risk levels, probabilities, and overall impact. Your team will help you formalize the Risk Management Plan by taking into account multiple factors, lessons learned, and eventualities.

Project Risk Management in Practice!

James understands that the Plan Risk Management process requires a team. In his case, this team has been nominated by his CEO. The team consists of five selected members, two subject matter experts, an external stakeholder, and a stakeholder with responsibilities. Together, they can begin working on the risk identification process.

This is the team that will help you increase the probability and impact of positive events and decrease the impact and probability of negative events.

Developing Your Risk Management Plan

Once you have effectively established your Risk Team and settled on the inputs that you need to supply them with, you can move on to the output for this process. Plan Risk Management only has one output—the Risk Management Plan.

A Risk Management Plan is a complete project lifecycle Risk Management Plan for your project. It ensures that there is shared understanding and application of the established terms and methods to be used.

It also goes a long way to define team roles and responsibilities while informing stakeholders of their level of involvement. An in-depth Risk Management Plan takes the time to focus on key people, tools, and business factors.

Business factors include any important constraints that need to be dealt with and outlined. This will touch on items such as priority of scope, costs, and time constraints. These factors need to be agreed upon in your meetings with decision makers, and they will become priorities that will affect your future risk activities.

Along with agreement, you need to establish how much effort your team will put into risk management based on the project's features and levels of complexity. Before plunging into business factor establishment, your team needs to be sorted out. That means considering risk attitudes, tolerances, and thresholds.

The most important component of this includes clearly defining risk management roles and responsibilities. This helps with managing expectations around roles and team hierarchy. Communication issues need to be considered along with methods of communicating risk. That means discussing, defining, and working out the communication details that will be used during the project.

Tools are the final consideration to be dealt with, and that means assessing the many tools that could be used to support or drive the Project Risk Management Process. Selecting and then outlining rules of use, definitions, and terms needs to be done for clarity. To ensure the greatest efficiency, the best tools and techniques must be matched with the right processes tailored to meet the unique circumstances of each project.

As your team develops the Risk Management Plan, you will need to take two distinct types of criteria into account: project- and process-related criteria. Project-related criteria focus on the required results for cost, scope, time, and quality and then examine the ways in which risk can impact these factors, especially the results they intend on producing.

Process-related criteria deal with the key processes that should be followed to attain success. Your team needs to ask themselves what risks exist that may impact the selected processes. Once you have discussed your Risk Management Plan at length and established your criteria, it will become part of your project baseline.

A project baseline[21] is the accepted and approved plan at a particular point in time during the project lifecycle. The baseline should be formally approved by management first and can be considered to be one of the key outputs of the planning stage. This baseline will enable you to objectively track project progress and to correctly forecast the outcomes.

---

21   Srinivasan Babou, What Are Project Baselines?, http://leadershipchamps. wordpress.com/2008/03/12/what-are-project-baselines/

Project Risk Management in Practice!

James has compiled a list of tasks that his team will need to perform to finally reach their Risk Management Plan determination.

- **Methods used:** Consider approach/tools/data/risk breakdown structure

- **Roles and Responsibilities:** Define lead support/team members/risk team

- **Scheduling:** Define when risk management will be conducted

- **Cost:** Define how risk will run alongside cost performance/ contingency plans

- **Risk Categories:** Define risk category impact and look at time, scope, quality, and cost

- **Define Probability/Impact:** Chance that a risk will occur/ consequences of risk

- **Stakeholders:** Level of risk/attitude factors/tolerance factors/threshold ranges

- **Tracking:** Recording/sharing/auditing/lessons captured

- **Reporting Formats:** Risk recording in reports/templates/ docs/communication

Important Terminology and Processes

Risk Breakdown Structure (RBS): Risk categories and sub-categories are listed in a hierarchy to help you identify risk. It defines specific risks that are applicable to projects being managed in that category.

Project Risk Management in Practice!

James has brought along his finance RBS for the use of his team. It clearly outlines low-, medium-, and high-risk project areas.

Finance Risk Breakdown Structure:

Feature	Low	Medium	High
Budget Size	Ideal budget allocation	Questionable budget allocation	Doubtful budget allocation
Cost	Costs known and set; will not exceed budget	Costs for some items not known	Cost analysis has not been done or estimates hard to glean
Return	Calculated to exceed financial criteria; large cash inflow early in project	Project returns within normal practices; cash flow continuous throughout project life	Returns on project subject to assumption & variances; uncertain cash flow, not easily measured
Cost controls	Established; fixed in place	System in place; some weakness	No system
Budget constraints	Funds allocated	Questions about fund availability	Funds in doubt or could change

You need to understand two key terms here: "assumptions" and "constraints." Because the risk management plan must contain a process to validate them, assumptions should be included; all things believed to be true must be analyzed periodically. Secondly, constraints need to be considered. These are the elements that could limit your team's solution options. They also define boundaries that need to be respected.

Review these key definitions:

- *Risk Threshold*: A measure of what level of risk your stakeholder is willing to accept. They are shown as figures or percentages and help determine responses to that risk.
- *Risk Averse*: This is a stakeholder's unwillingness to accept higher levels of uncertainty or risk.
- *Risk Tolerance Areas*: Because key stakeholders will accept risk in these areas, they need to be properly defined and identified.
- *Risk Utility*: This describes an individual's or organization's willingness to accept risk.
- *Define your project's objectives*: Include time, cost, scope, and quality as well as other relevant metrics.
- *Share your risk management plan*: Stakeholders must agree so that it becomes part of your project management plan.
- *Find and address obstacles*: Identify anything that could impact the risk management plan.
- *Stakeholder Involvement*: You need perspectives from stakeholders and multiple sources. Work towards obtaining their buy-in.
- *Organizational Process Assets*: Secure important templates, records, and lessons learned to understand and leverage them. Make relevant inputs from previous projects and phases available to your team.
- *Compliance*: Make sure all policies and procedures are followed. Adhere to key governance criteria and methods.
- *Categorization*: Categorize risks to group them based on common causes. This makes risk response easier.

Study Success: 10 Sample Questions

Based on the information you have learned about Plan Risk Management, answer the following questions:

What term is used to describe the following?

1. *The essential tool and technique used to plan risk management and generate your required outputs*

2. *Factors that limit a Risk Team's options*

3. *An individual's or organization's willingness to accept risk*

4. *An essential input in Plan Risk Management that includes templates, stakeholder information, policies, and procedures*

Answer the following questions:

5. *What is the step that must be taken before establishing a project baseline?*

6. *What does PIER-C stand for?*

7. *Name 5 inputs for Plan Risk Management.*

8. *Define the function of a Risk Breakdown Structure.*

9. *What 3 things does a Risk Management Plan address?*

10. *What is the single deliverable that will define the overall strategy to be used to support the Risk Management Process.*

Answers:

Answer 1: Planning Meetings and Analysis

Answer 2: Constraints

Answer 3: Risk Utility

Answer 4: Organizational Process Assets

Answer 5: Submit your plan to management for approval.

Answer 6: Plan risk management, Identify risks, Evaluate (Qualitative and Quantitative Risk Analysis), Plan risk responses, and Control risks

Answer 7: Project management plan, project charter, stakeholder register, enterprise environmental factors, and organizational process assets

Answer 8: An RBS places risks in categories and defines how specific risks are applicable to the type of project being managed.

Answer 9: It addresses the risks involved with people, tools, and business factors.

Answer 10: A Risk Management Plan

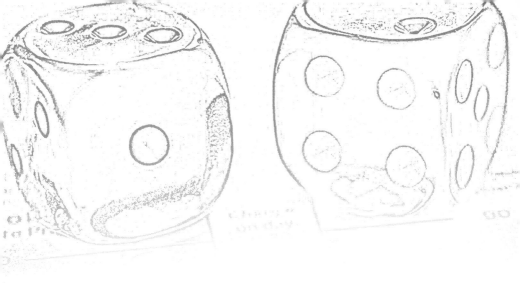

CHAPTER 5

IDENTIFY RISKS

"Managing an organization's risks in individual silos is like trying to pick up a six-pack without the little plastic thingy that holds them all together; you can do it, but it is far harder than it would be if the cans were connected to each other."

ANDREW BENT

PIER-C: The second process in the Project Risk Management Knowledge Area is to Identify Risks. It focuses on your role in developing a list of risks that are segmented into specific areas—for example, by category, work package, or activity. It is during this step that you will clearly define risks, assign ownership to them, and then seek to define the cause of risks.

Your project team will also need to develop the initial responses to risks and then categorize each risk so that it can be effectively dealt with. The core output for identifying risk is to formulate a document that is known as a "Risk Register." A Risk Register initially records identified risks and their characteristics.

How to Identify Risks

In this second critical process, you will create the first version of your Risk Register. The Risk Register should include the Risk Owner, category, risk, causes, triggers, and first line response. It is called the "initial iteration" of the Risk Register and does not yet include your Risk Scores, priorities, analysis, or a detailed response plan.

All risks should have a specific, single owner. This "Risk Owner" will be validated and potentially altered as the Plan Risk Responses activities are performed. You, as the project manager, will act as the stand-in Risk Owner if no other team member is put forward.

A Risk Register[22] can be defined as a risk management tool that is commonly used in project management and organizational risk assessments. It is a central place where all risks can be identified by the project team and where each of these risks includes their own pertinent factors; namely, who the Risk Owner is, countermeasures to be taken, risk probability, and impact.

Any number of risks can be outlined; there is no cap. The general rule is that "more is better" because it pays to be thorough when risk is concerned. When you begin with the Identify Risks process, you should ensure that multiple stakeholders are actively involved to include their input. [2223]

Your team members should also offer insight into the Identify Risks process. This way, stakeholders and your Risk Team will have a sense of ownership and will feel responsible for managing these outlined risks. The Risk Register is a very important input for all of your Risk Management Processes moving forward. It will need to be updated consistently as the Risk Management Processes proceed, working its way through PIER-C. When you create a Risk Register, it becomes an iterative practice.

Risk Meta Language[23] is the method that enables you to identify and describe risk using a three-step method to develop a risk statement—cause, risk, and effect; for example, minimum stakeholder commitment (cause), poor scope statement acceptance (uncertain event/risk), causing schedule delays (effect).

22   Risk Register, Wikipedia, http://en.wikipedia.org/wiki/Risk_register

23   David Hillson, Using Risk Metalanguage to Develop Risk Responses, http://www.risk-doctor.com/pdf-briefings/risk-doctor22e.pdf

Identify Risks Process Explained

The method for identifying risks also includes using inputs, tools and techniques, and outputs. Identify Risks[24] is the process of determining the risks that may potentially prevent your program, investment, project, or enterprise from achieving its objectives. It includes documenting and communicating these risks.

Management of risks is an ongoing process, which means that risks can change during the project. For example, the environment may be altered, which could impact risks in your project. Identifying risks is therefore carried out consistently through the project; creating a Risk Register is just the initial step.

Your Risk Register will eventually feed the subsequent four risk management processes, so it is important that the project team considers it to be a vital stage of the process. General control of risks is usually achieved by selecting from the hierarchy of control measures, one or more of which can individually, or in combination, achieve the required risk reduction.

All projects have risks, and it is your job to identify them as part of the Identify Risks process. Risk identification is an integrative process that requires active stakeholder engagement; participation will vary from project to project or cycle to cycle. The risk tolerance of stakeholders is significant as the risk identification process leads to the qualitative risk analysis process.

Project Risk Management in Practice!

James needs to lay out the inputs, tools and techniques, and outputs that this process requires to clearly illustrate the flow.

---

24 Risk Identification, http://www.mitre.org/publications/systems-engineering-guide/acquisition-systems-engineering/risk-management/risk-identification

Inputs	Tools & Techniques	Outputs
• Risk management plan • Cost management plan	• Documentation reviews	• Initial Risk Register
• Schedule management plan • Quality management plan • Human resource management plan • Scope baseline • Activity cost estimates • Activity duration estimates • Stakeholder register • Project documents • Procurement documents • Enterprise environmental factors • Organizational process assets	• Information-gathering techniques • Checklist analysis • Assumptions analysis • Diagramming techniques • SWOT analysis • Expert judgement	

Inputs and Outputs Involved in Identify Risks

The inputs and outputs involved in risk identification are straightforward and should be understood. At the beginning of your risk identification process, you need to list key inputs along with their applicability to your project.

- *Risk Management Plan*: This helps in defining your processes and strategy so that you can achieve end-to-end Project Risk Management. It defines your method, your role, and the roles of your team members. It also identifies the available resources via the RBS.

- *Cost Management Plan*: The cost management plan defines how your contingency reserves are estimated, reported, and eventually assessed. It will also help you outline your approach to cost risk management.

- *Schedule Management Plan:* The schedule management plan defines how your schedule contingencies will be estimated, assessed, and reported on. They will also define how you and your team will respond to time risk management during the project.

- *Quality Management Plan:* Your quality management plan[25] will define a specific approach to quality. This may include metrics, standards, checklists for quality control, targets, and process improvement opportunities that you identify.

- *Human Resource Management Plan:* This plan provides guidance on how project human resources should be defined, staffed, managed, and eventually released. It also covers roles and responsibilities, which becomes critical to managing risks effectively.

- *Scope Baseline:* The scope baseline includes the project scope statement, the work breakdown structure (WBS), and the WBS dictionary. The scope statement includes a list of assumptions. The WBS helps communicate the project deliverables in a summary format and is decomposed into work packages.

- *Activity Cost Estimates:* Activity cost estimates are necessary because where there are cost estimates, there is risk. You need to consider your stakeholder tolerances and thresholds when these costs are going to be estimated.

- *Activity Duration Estimates:* To reiterate, where activity duration estimates exist, there is inherent risk. Once again, you need to consider your stakeholder tolerances and thresholds to reduce the risk involved.

- *Stakeholder Register:* This is a register that contains important information on your stakeholders, such as

---

25 Identify Risks Process, http://www.pm-primer.com/identify-risks/

their identification information, classification as to status (internal, external, supporter, or neutral), and assessment information, including requirements, interest, influence, and expectations for alignment.

- **Project Documents:** Your project documents include your assumptions log, earned value technique metrics, work performance reports, baselines, and any network diagrams that are relevant.

- **Procurement Documents:** Procurement documents become a key input for identifying risks if the project requires external procurement of resources.

- **Enterprise Environmental Factors:** This includes your studies, checklists, published information, industry studies, benchmarking, and risk attitudes that are pertinent to the project.

- **Organizational Process Assets:** These will include your project documents, controls, lessons learned, historical information, and, of course, your templates.

Once your inputs are in order and you leverage the recommended tools and techniques, you will produce a Risk Register. This Risk Register becomes part of your formal project management plan when it is approved and accepted.

The Risk Register will be periodically updated as the project moves forward; it becomes an input for subsequent Risk Management processes. The main entries that are recommended for inclusion in your Risk Register are as follows:

Project Risk Management in Practice!

James has outlined his Risk Register, and it looks like this:

Risk	Causes & Triggers	Risk Owner	Category	Risk Response

- Understand the definition of risk, event, and consequence.
- Understand the causes of and triggers for each individual risk.
- Understand who the initial risk owners are.
- Understand risk categorization.
- Understand risk response.

Many of these sections will be worked on at a later stage in the PIER-C.

Strategies, Tools and Techniques

Once you fully understand the inputs of identifying risks, you will need to know how to leverage these tools and techniques to create the Risk Register. This requires looking at previous project records and the current project work performance data as well as project forecasts.

As a project risk manager, for example, you would use historical information and compare it with current and other past projects. This will equip you with information that can be valuable in identifying risks, issues, and benefits. Leverage the experience of team members to help identify risks.

James has compiled the following important documents to help make informed decisions:

- Documentation reviews
- Information gathering techniques, which include:
  - Brainstorming
  - Interviews
  - Root Cause Analysis
  - Delphi Technique
- Checklist analysis
- Assumptions analysis
- Diagramming techniques
- Cause and effect diagrams
- Influence diagrams
- SWOT analysis

Learn the definition of each to fully understand the process of converting inputs into the Risk Register using these specific tools and techniques.

- ***Documentation Reviews*:** A documentation review requires that you read through all of your project documentation to ensure that it is easily understood and clear. Check to be sure your documented methods match your project goals and that all of these documents are reviewed and edited and clearly communicate information to stakeholders.
- ***Information Gathering Techniques*:** There are several potential methods that PMI recommends for information gathering, and the exam will contain many questions

from this area. These tools and techniques need to be understood and leveraged by project managers.

- *Brainstorming*: A brainstorming session[26] is an open forum in which team members can generate ideas and come up with potential solutions. Someone usually logs inputs during this process. Brainstorming is a method of attaining expert input, but the team must avoid evaluating responses during the session.

- *Interviews*: Interviews with stakeholders and experts in a specific field can provide a great deal of information; it can, however, be a time-consuming process.

- *Root Cause Analysis*: Root cause analysis groups risks by common causes, which aids in developing more effective risk responses.

- *Delphi Technique*: This technique attains inputs and a common consensus through the use of anonymous input from experts, which reduces the bandwagon or halo effects. Surveys and questionnaires are two common methods used to solicit information. The main goal here is to share the end results with everyone. This knowledge-sharing allows experts to expand their knowledge base, and feedback will identify even more risks. The Delphi Technique provides social intelligence without the intimidation factors that can hamper open discussion.

- *Nominal Group Technique*: After brainstorming, the list is ranked and prioritized. The goal is problem identification, solution generation, and group decision making.

---

26   Institute of Management Accountants, Enterprise Risk Management: Tools and Techniques for Effective Implementation, http://erm.ncsu.edu/az/erm/i/chan/m-articles/documents/IMAToolsTechniquesMay07.pdf

- *Checklist Analysis*: A checklist analysis is made up of the lessons learned that allow you to create lists that support a number of different projects. When you use a checklist analysis approach, it helps you identify the potential risks so that you can plan ahead for them. This simple approach is used to perform an initial high-level analysis of risks. It does not identify new risks that are not on the generic checklist.

- *Assumptions Analysis*: An assumptions analysis must be done for every project. Assumptions are risks waiting to happen. All assumptions must be validated or dismissed before moving forward.

- *Diagramming Techniques*: PMI recommends several diagramming techniques that can be used to identify risks. These often support the project quality management process and include a few of the following diagrams.

  - *Cause and Effect Diagrams*: A cause and effect diagram shows the potential risk factor for that cause and the effect that it may bring about. These are also called Fishbone Diagrams or Ishikawa Diagrams.

  - *Influence Diagrams*: This diagramming method includes graphical representation of situations that show causal influences, time ordering of events, and other types of relationships between variables and potential outcomes.

  - *System or Process Flow Charts*: All project managers should understand how to map and analyze processes. A process flow chart shows how systems function and interrelate and serves as a means for identifying potential risk.

  - *Affinity Diagramming*: This tool is commonly used to organize a large number of ideas stemming from brainstorming into a group. This is a useful method to use when your team believes that not all risks have been correctly identified.

◆ **FMEA**: Failure Modes and Effect Analysis is another tool that helps in the identification of potential failure modes by determining the effect of each failure. It involves reviewing as many components, assemblies, and subsystems as possible to identify failure modes and their causes and effects.

• **SWOT Analysis**: A linchpin in any analysis, SWOT analyses opportunities and threats are based on common strengths and weaknesses. Strengths and weaknesses are often internal, while opportunities and threats are usually external. Strengths often lead to better opportunities or positive risks. Weaknesses do the opposite.

You will lead your team in correctly identifying the appropriate tools and techniques to use when identifying risks.

Developing Your Ability to Identify Risks

Your ability to identify risks is directly related to your knowledge of the tools and techniques that can be used to discover them. In order to hone your skills as a project risk manager, you will need to focus on some key areas for development.

• *Your sources matter:* In order to correctly identify risks,[27] you must utilize multiple sources of information. The more information you use, the better oriented you will be. Get inputs from multiple stakeholders so that you can secure multiple perspectives.

---

27   Risk Identification Methods - 12 Types, https://manager.clearrisk.com/ Resources/RiskTool/Risk_Identification_Methods_-_12_Types

- *Frequency of analysis is important*: I have already mentioned that the process of identifying risks is an ongoing one— meaning that it is a recurring or iterative process. You must periodically repeat this process when it adds value to do so. Risks are waiting to be identified, so be aware of this as you move through your project.

- *Your timing is critical*: You should identify project risks very early in your project to ensure success. When you know about risks, they can be analyzed and responded to. Any unknown risk can catch you and your stakeholders by surprise. Risk is there whether you find and prepare for it or not, so take an approach that enhances your chances of identifying the majority of the risks.

- *Risk statements matter*: The best risk definitions use risk meta-language methods of cause and effect. The goals are to reduce ambiguity and increase the level of detail.

- *New risk validation must be done*: You need as much information as possible to clearly define any new risks that are reported. Share these new risks with your team and stakeholders so that you can learn as much as possible about the cause and effect for each respective risk.

- *Always link risks to objectives*: Every single risk could have the potential to impact a key project objective, whether it is scope, time, cost, or quality.

- *Visibility is a concern*: Your Risk Register must be available to all project stakeholders for review. It needs to be used as a primary tool to review risks at periodic meetings when project status is discussed.

- *Risk types matter*: You need to identify both positive and negative risks; do not dwell on the negative risks only. Include the positive risks or opportunities as well.

- *Ownership is critical*: Initial Risk Owners will be assigned at this stage. Each risk needs to have an owner, and there should only be one Risk Owner for each risk. In other words, every agreed upon and funded risk response needs an owner.

These factors matter when you are learning to develop your team and your processes for risk identification. Focus on them and you will improve the percentage of risk you discover and the quality of analysis that goes into determining potential responses later on.

Study Success: 10 Sample Questions

Based on the information you have learned about Identifying Risk, answer the following questions.

What term is used to describe the following?

1. *Similar to brainstorming, input is collected from a specific group, which is then analyzed and rank ordered by the group.*

2. *This type of diagram method includes graphical representations of situations that show causal influences, time ordering of events, and other types of relationships between variables and potential outcomes.*

3. *This defines how your risk budget and contingency reserves are reported and eventually assessed. It will also help you define your approach to cost management as a function.*

4. *This includes your assumptions log, earned value technique metrics, work performance reports, baselines, and any network diagrams that are relevant.*

5. *Name the 5 Risk Register categories you need to understand.*

6. *Name the 13 inputs for identifying risk.*

7. *Define Risk Register.*

8. *Why is frequency of analysis important?*

9. *What does a scope baseline include?*

10. *Name 4 tools and techniques used in Identifying Risk.*

Answers:

Answer 1: Nominal group technique

Answer 2: Influence diagrams

Answer 3: Cost management plan

Answer 4: Project documents

Answer 5: Understand the definition of risk and of event and consequence, causes, and triggers for each individual risk, who the initial risk owners are, risk categorization, and risk response.

Answer 6: Risk management plan, Activity cost estimates, Activity duration estimates, Scope baseline, Stakeholder register, Cost management plan, Schedule management plan, Human resource management plan, Quality management plan, Procurement documents,

Project documents, Enterprise environmental factors, and Organizational process assets

Answer 7: A Risk Register can be defined as a risk management tool that is commonly used in project management and organizational risk assessments. It is a central place where all risks can be identified by the project team, and each of these risks includes their own number of factors; namely, who the Risk Owner is, counter measures to be taken, risk probability, and impact.

Answer 8: You must repeat this process periodically when it adds value to do so. Risks are waiting to be identified, so be aware of this as you move through your project.

Answer 9: The scope baseline includes your scope statement, WBS, and the WBS dictionary. The scope statement is a list of assumptions. The WBS helps define the activities in a summary, in work package levels, or as a control account.

Answer 10: Documentation reviews, information gathering techniques, Checklist analysis, or Assumptions analysis (or any of these: Diagramming techniques, SWOT analysis, etc.)

CHAPTER 6

PERFORM QUALITATIVE RISK ANALYSIS

"Get the right people. Then no matter what all else you might do wrong after that, the people will save you. That's what management is all about."

TOM DEMARCO

PIER-C: Once you understand the fundamentals and have worked through Plan Risk Management and Identify Risks, you start the Evaluation process. Performing Qualitative Risk Analysis is a subjective process. When you arrive at this step, you will use your Risk Register created during the Identification stage.

With the Risk Register, you will be able to classify risk by probability (the likelihood that the risk will happen) and the impact or effect the risk consequence will have on your specific project. By the time you complete this step, you will be able to prioritize risks and build a short, prioritized list of the risks that need to be actively managed.

This important output is known as the Urgent List. You will also sort low probability and impact risks into a different part of your Risk Register, called a Watch List. During this critical process, your Risk Register will be updated with this new information.

What Is Qualitative Risk Analysis?

As the third step in the Risk Management journey, this process aims to prioritize any further actions. These qualitative risk analysis results are subjective. The Risk Management Plan and Risk Register are used in this analysis to assess the probability and impact of each individual risk.

Defined, a qualitative risk analysis[28] is the process of prioritizing risks for further analysis or action by assessing and combining their probability of occurrence and impact. It assesses the priority of identified risks using their probability of occurring and the corresponding impact as well as other factors, like time frame and risk tolerance.

The end goal for the Qualitative Risk Analysis is to update your Risk Register, which is a constant work in progress. You need to consider the causes of risks when you calculate probability and impact. It is fairly common for a single cause to result in multiple potential events which, in turn, cause multiple consequences.

Path convergence[29] can be defined as multiple activities flowing into or from a central activity. To consolidate effort and remove redundancy, sometimes combining series or items is needed. For example, a project management team might merge a number of parallel schedule network paths into the same point.

Path convergence happens when the team characterizes a pre-existing schedule activity into more than one predecessor activity. As the project unfolds, path convergence happens—it can cause some confusion, so it needs to be handled carefully by the team lead or project risk manager. Path divergence refers to a situation where the project management team generates parallel schedule network paths from the same node.

---

28   Qualitative Risk Analysis, http://www.mypmps.net/en/mypmps/knowledgeareas/risk/qualitative-risk-analysis.html
29   Project Management Knowledge, Path Convergence, http://project-management-knowledge.com/definitions/p/path-convergence/

How to Perform Qualitative Risk Analysis

Elaborating on path convergence, a project network diagram will show the dependencies for all activities and will identify where these paths converge. You can see this in the unit below as multiple activities flow from Exercise A.

Project Risk Management in Practice!

You can see larger levels of path convergence increase risk probability and impact here. Exercises B, C, and D rely on the completion of Exercise A. If a risk impacts Exercise A, there is much greater risk to the project because of the related convergences.

Performing qualitative risk analysis[30] relies on these exercises to uncover hidden risks and correctly prioritize them. First, the project manager will analyze the risks that have been identified in the previous steps. These risks will be assessed for probability and impact in the project, one by one. It is a fairly fast process because these risk factors need to be uncovered quickly.

---

30   Qualitative Risk Analysis and How to Perform It, http://www.pm-primer.com/perform-qualitative-risk-analysis/

At the very top of any project manager's list is the discovery and establishment of highest priority risk items. The probability and impact matrix is used to prioritize and tier tasks by importance, and the information is eventually fed back into the Risk Register.

Keep in mind that not all risk is the same, so the tiering or ranking process of all known risks is imperative. You need to know the best time and resources to match to the appropriate tasks within the project as soon as possible.

Remember that qualitative risk analysis is performed several times during a project so that the Risk Register is kept fresh and usable. Making subjective judgments on these risks means understanding how each risk is likely to occur and, if it does, how it would affect the project.

Qualitative risk analysis is a popular, quick, and cost-effective method of prioritizing tasks. Its core benefit is that it allows you to reduce the levels of uncertainty about your project and to focus your efforts on critical areas of high priority risks.

The Qualitative Risk Analysis Process Explained

To correctly perform a qualitative risk analysis, you need to work through the process of finding inputs and using the right tools and techniques to convert them into the desired outputs. The process is quick and easy, but it needs to be consistent.

You can see in the above table that all of the core input documentation is used—the Risk Management Plan continues to evolve along with the Risk Register, the Scope Baseline, and your set of Organizational Process Assets. These continue to inform you and your team so that you can apply the correct tools in this three-step process.

Project Risk Management in Practice!

James and his team need to perform the qualitative risk analysis process, so they have outlined their inputs, tools and techniques, and outputs for use.

Inputs	Tools & Techniques	Outputs
• Risk management plan • Scope baseline • Risk register • Enterprise environmental factors • Organizational process assets	• Risk Probability and Impact Assessment • Probability and Impact Matrix • Risk Data Quality Assessment • Risk Categorization • Risk Urgency Assessment • Expert judgment	• Project documents updates

Once your inputs are finalized via the risk identification process, you will select the tools and techniques that you will need to progress your project. In qualitative risk analysis,[31] this means executing Risk Probability and Impact Assessments, building Probability and Impact Matrixes, creating Risk Data Quality Assessments, applying Risk Categorization, and conducting Risk Urgency Assessments. Expert judgment is heavily relied upon in this process.

Remember that once you have used all of these tools and techniques, your end goal is to update your Risk Register with the new information. Keeping updated documents fuels your strategy and keeps your project team on target based on the Risk Management Plan.

---

31   Perform Qualitative Risk Analysis, http://www.testeagle.com/classroom/
sample-lesson-perform-qualitative-risk-analysis.aspx

Inputs to Consider With Qualitative Risk Analysis

Now that you have reached the input level again, you can take a look at your two previous outputs from Plan Risk Management and Risk Identification. Your Risk Management Plan is the output from your Plan Risk Management stage, and the Risk Register is the output from the Identify Risks process.

This qualitative step cannot be conducted without both outputs from the two previous sections. Project Risk Management steps are therefore all interrelated, and the integrity of one fuels the next to ensure competent strategy and continuous improvement.

James has compiled the following five inputs to use in qualitative risk analysis:

- Risk Management Plan
- Scope Baseline
- Risk Register
- Enterprise Environmental Factors
- Organizational Process Assets

Learn the definition of each to fully understand the process of converting these inputs into value added project document updates as outputs.

- ***Risk Management Plan:*** This defines the responsibilities, roles, and methods[32] used to evaluate risk in its entirety. It also serves to provide core definitions for probability

---

32 5th Edition PMBOK Guide: Chapter 11: Process 11.3 Perform Qualitative Risk Analysis, http://4squareviews.com/2013/08/01/5th-edition-pmbok-guide-chapter-11-process-11-3-perform-qualitative-risk-analysis/

and impact that lies at the heart of this stage. The Risk Management Plan is the framework for all of these processes.

- *Scope Baseline*: Projects that are common or are recurrent in nature generally are better understood by the project team. Highly complex projects, as well as innovative projects where new technologies and research are being tried out, tend to have a higher level of uncertainty. The scope baseline assists with evaluating the level of uncertainty

- *Risk Register*: The Risk Register provides the initial list of risks that will need to be evaluated. This critical document will be updated regularly at multiple intervals as the project moves forward and will include the current qualitative analysis. It may also contain some Risk Responses that have already been identified and sorted out.

- *Enterprise Environmental Factors*: Enterprise environmental factors may provide information that helps put the risks in context.

- *Organizational Process Assets*: Organizational Process Assets include risk databases, lessons learned from past strategies, templates, studies from previous projects, and historical information and could include Risk Rating rules. This information on past project risks can be an exceptionally useful input at this stage.

With these main inputs, you will be able to apply your tools and techniques to make educated decisions about risk using various types of models and assessments. It is very important that up until this point, your information has been informative and instructional—although it will require subjective discussion at many junctures. Other inputs could easily be added, depending on your project, but most of them will fall into these main categories.

Strategies, Tools and Techniques

Qualitative risk analysis is both quick and easy and, as a method for prioritizing risks on the Risk Register, highly effective. To illustrate this process, we will return to James and his Risk Team.

James has compiled the following tools and techniques to perform qualitative risk analysis with his team:

- Risk Probability and Impact Assessment
- Probability and Impact Matrix
- Risk Data Quality Assessment
- Risk Categorization
- Risk Urgency Assessment
- Expert Judgment

Learn the definition of each to fully understand the process of converting the selected inputs using these tools and techniques into the desired outputs.

- ***Risk Probability and Impact Assessment***: As a rule, all risks should be evaluated on individual merit and scored for probability/likelihood and impact/effect. Creating a consistent scoring system will ensure that all risks are analyzed in the same manner. The Risk Management Plan should already contain the values needed for probability and risk, so take them from there. Qualitative descriptions[33] of characteristics can range from very low to very high.

---

33   Risk Management 11.3 Perform Qualitative Risk Analysis, http://anamulhuq. blogspot.com/2012/01/risk-managment-113-perform-qualitative.html

- **Probability:** This is concerned with the potential for risk to occur. Probability is therefore calculated using scoring systems like percentages or numeric scales. These assigned scores are called Risk Ratings. If they are too high, you will have to find a way to remove the cause of that risk. The term used for this process is avoidance.
- **Impact:** This refers to the consequences that the risk will have on the project should the event ever happen. Because your primary objectives concern scope, quality, cost, and time, you need to score your impact based on project-specific factors. Many project managers use weighted impact ratings that will assign higher values to higher risks. For example, if cost is the main priority, risks that impact cost plans will be of a higher rank. Numeric scores here are also called Risk Ratings.
- **Risk Score:** To determine your Risk Score, you will need to multiply probability and impact (probability × impact). Risk Scores help you determine if risk responses are developed as well as how detailed each risk response should be. High risk scores mean high levels of response; low risk scores mean low levels of response.

Risk	Probability Risk Rating	Impact Risk Rating	Risk Score
A	4	4	16
B	3	4	12
C	2	4	8
D	1	5	5

You can see in the table above that "A" has the highest priority because it has received the highest score—simple. The lowest is D for the same reason, even though it has a high impact score.

Probability and Impact Matrix: Your company may have an existing probability and impact matrix, or, as the project manager, you may have to develop a standard one for your team. It shows the risk ratings and overall priority of all risks. These can be as simple as you like or as complex as required depending on the method you choose.

Probability & Impact Scoring	Low Probability	Moderate Probability	High Probability
Low Impact	1	2	3
Moderate Impact	2	4	6
High Impact	3	6	9
Assign all risks with a score of 4 or less to the Watch List. Develop responses for risks that have a score of 6 of more for adequate planning.			

The tool above is sometimes called a Lookup Table and focuses on high priority risks because they can rapidly improve overall project performance. When you describe your Risk Rating criteria and develop a probability and impact matrix, it will reduce your potential for bias and improve the quality of your analysis.

- ***Risk Data Quality Assessment:*** You need to review the data used to determine the probability and that impact scores are accurate and unbiased. The data that are used might not be enough to accurately define your Risk Score. If that is true, you need to gather more information to improve your understanding before submitting your final analysis. Always correct a risk assessment that contains bias.

- *Motivational, Cognitive, and Desired Bias*: There are three main types of biases to watch out for. Motivational bias happens when stakeholders intentionally attempt to bias Risk Ratings one way or the other. Cognitive bias stems from a skewed perception of reality. Finally, desired bias is when it might make sense to be biased towards high priority risk—like the cost plan bias spoken about earlier. The best way to reduce biases is via qualitative risk analysis in order to define levels of probability and impact.

- *Risk Categorization*: Risk categorization refers to grouping risk by category so that defining risk responses becomes easier as the Risk Management Process goes on. Determining common causes that could impact multiple risks is part of this vital practice.

- *Risk Urgency Assessment:*[34] When this qualitative risk analysis process has been completed, you will be left with a prioritized list of risks. Questions to which you must respond include: Which risks should be immediately addressed? Which risks go on the Watch List? This assessment prioritizes your risk response activity.

- The Risks found to be immediate are placed on the Urgent List with a Risk Rating that denotes the level of urgency. The list may be based on quality, scope, time, and/or cost objectives. Risks that do not require immediate response are placed on the Watch List; they have a low Risk Score and are "accepted" as being short term.

---

34   Risk Urgency Assessment, http://getpmpcertified.blogspot.com/2013/01/risk-urgency-assessment.html

Study Success: 5 Sample Questions

Based on the information you have learned about Qualitative Risk Analysis, answer the following questions.

What term is used to describe the following?

1. *This is concerned with the potential for risks to occur. It is therefore calculated using scoring systems like percentages or numeric scales. These assigned scores are called Risk Ratings. If they are too high, you will have to find a way to remove the cause of that risk. The term used for describing this process is avoidance.*

2. *Multiple activities flowing into or from a central activity. To consolidate effort and remove redundancy, combining series or items is sometimes needed; an example would be when a project management team merges a number of parallel schedule network paths into the same point.*

3. *To determine this, you need to multiply probability and impact (probability × impact). This will help you learn if risk responses are developed as well as how detailed each risk response should be. High risk scores mean high levels of response; low risk scores mean low levels of response.*

4. *Your company may have an existing probability and impact matrix or, as the project manager, you may have to develop a*

standard one for your team. It shows the risk ratings and overall priority of all risks. These can be as simple as you like or as complex as required depending on the method you choose.

5. *When this qualitative risk analysis process has been completed, you will be left with a prioritized list of risks. Questions to which you must respond include: Which risks should be immediately addressed? Which risks go on the Watch List? This assessment prioritizes your risk response activity.*

Answers:

Answer 1: Probability

Answer 2: Path convergence

Answer 3: Risk Score

Answer 4: Probability and Impact Matrix

Answer 5: Risk Urgency Assessment

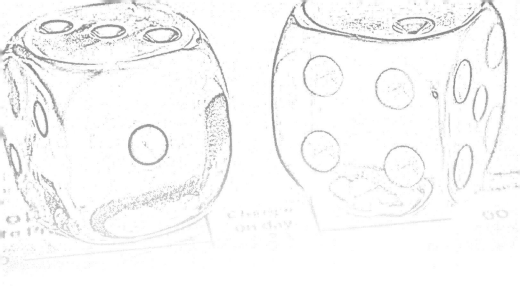

CHAPTER 7

PERFORM QUALITATIVE RISK ANALYSIS

"There is a continuum between certainty and uncertainty, just as there is between factors inside and outside of our control. By studying the uncertain, we may be able to break it down into elements of greater and lesser risk, of greater and lesser predictability. In the same way, between absolute control and absence of control lies the middle ground of influence and persuasion."

CHANTELL ILBURY & CLEM SUNTER

PIER-C: We will now look at the second part of Performing Qualitative Risk Analysis as outlined in the previous chapter. Again, the subjective process continues with the development of an Urgent List and Watch List; when completed, your Risk Register will be updated.

The Outputs Involved in Qualitative Risk Analysis

After you have carefully worked through the Perform Qualitative Risk Analysis process, you will be left with an updated Risk Register. This will contain a host of things that will help drive your analysis forward into the next stage of Risk Management planning.

To better understand the outputs from this analysis, we will return to our project manager, James, and his team to see how they are updating the relevant project risk documents.

- *Project Document Updates*: This is the main output of qualitative risk analysis. It includes but is not limited to risk register updates and assumptions log updates.
- *Risk Ratings*: Ranking or prioritizing risk is done by adding Risk Ratings to your Risk Register. All risks should be added this way so that each risk probability and impact is assigned a Risk Rating. Do not forget to multiply the probability and impact Risk Ratings to achieve your Risk Score.

James has compiled the following outputs resulting from qualitative risk analysis:

- Updating the Risk Register
- Risk Ratings
- Project Risk Score
- Category Grouping
- Urgent List
- Additional Analysis
- Watch Lists
- Risk Trends

Learn the definition of each to fully understand the process of achieving these outputs by correctly selecting inputs and tools and techniques and using them to inform your outcome.

- *Project Risk Score*: To calculate the overall project Risk Score to keep a running number, you need to add all the individual Risk Scores together, which will result in a figure that reflects your Project Risk Score. When this is complete, you can calculate your Risk Exposure, which is based on your Project Risk Score, a term that refers to the level of risk in your project. As is always the case, acceptable levels of Risk Exposure are based on stakeholder thresholds, tolerances, and attitudes.

Probability × Impact Risk Ratings = Risk Score

Probability × Impact Risk Ratings = Risk Score

Total Amount of Combined Risk Scores = Project Risk Score

Project Risk Scores = Risk Exposure Calculation

If, for example, Project 1 had a Risk Score of 125 and established acceptable levels of Risk Exposure were defined as projects with a Risk Exposure level less than 90, the project manager must step in to lower this Risk Score. If there is no way to lower the score, the Risk Score may lead to a "No Go" decision on the project.

- *Category Grouping*: Revisiting the grouping of risks by category helps with progressive elaboration of the categorization that was completed during the Identify Risks process.
- *Urgent List*: Remember, your Risk Register will contain risks that require immediate responses; these are placed on the Urgent List. The highest risk score takes priority; the higher the Risk Score, the more urgent the issue.
- *Additional Analysis*: Sometimes risks do need further analysis; scoring certain risks requires additional information.
- *Watch Lists*: Keep in mind that your Risk Register will contain low priority risks that do not require immediate attention. The project manager is usually the owner of these risks, which means that you need to watch them in case their scores increase.
- *Risk Trends*: Asking yourself about risk trends can lead to new discoveries; for example, more risks developing in a specific category could be an indication of trouble. The figure below illustrates how a Risk Register changes when the Qualitative Risk Analysis process is complete.

Risk	Cause	Risk Owner	Category	Risk Response	Probability Risk Rating	Impact Risk Rating	Risk Score
		Initial		Initial	Step 3 addition	Step 3 addition	Step 3 addition

Urgent List for High Priority Risk							
					Risk rating in project: Where the risk is prioritized based on the risk score.		
Draw a line on the Risk Register at the conclusion to perform qualitative risk analysis. Risks that are high priority are placed on the Urgent List, and responses are developed for them. Low priority risks are put on the Watch List, and responses are only developed if the risk scores increase.							
Watch List For Low Priority Risk							
					Project risk score = total risk scores		

- Step 3 is where your Perform Qualitative Analysis process goes.
- Your project team and you will decide what needs to be included here. For the test, however, please focus on the given formats and entries.
- Two of the most powerful methods for performing qualitative risk analysis are conducting interviews and meetings.

When Will You Need to Use Qualitative Risk Analysis?

It is true that the risk assessment field is becoming more complex and multi-layered because of the methods used when assessing costs, auditing, compliance, and operations impacted by projects. There may be many factors within a project that need to receive a Risk Rating, so prepare to work with large amounts of data and scoring for practical purposes.

You will need to actively employ the tools and techniques of performing qualitative risk analysis once you have established the finalized inputs, which are actually outputs from the two previous processes—Identify Risks and Plan Risk Management.

The use of qualitative risk analysis[35] makes it easy to define intransient concepts like probability and impact by establishing numerical scores for improved accuracy in creating hierarchical, prioritized lists. If these lists do not have correct priorities and scores, risks that may disrupt the project could go unnoticed until it is too late.

By defining, scoring, and arranging these risk lists using qualitative risk analysis, you equip your team with readable tables and lists that can be used and updated throughout the Risk Process for both monitoring and management. Qualitative risk analysis typically comes before quantitative risk analysis. In most projects, quantitative risk analysis cannot be conducted as cost effectively without having first completed qualitative risk analysis.

Therefore, qualitative risk analysis also becomes a driving process in Project Risk Management. Immediately after completing your Identify Risks process, you will begin this type of analysis to improve accuracy and eliminate redundancies and bias.

In addition, Qualitative Risk Analysis is *always* done when a *new* risk is discovered. Even if you have had no new data for the last six months, the moment a new risk arises, the next natural step is to perform a qualitative risk analysis. You will need to score your new risks, define them, and then add them to your prioritized list.

If you fail to update your lists after new risks are discovered, those lists become out of date and your plan becomes ineffective. Consistent updating is required because of the long-term discovery of risks and their integration into an existing and ongoing strategy.

---

35   Qualitative Risk Analysis and Assessment, http://www.project-management-skills.com/qualitative-risk-analysis.html

The Qualitative Risk Analysis Success Roadmap

As a project risk manager, there are a number of things that you should keep in mind to ensure successful qualitative risk analysis. This roadmap will help steer you in the right direction moving forward.

- Probability and Impact Scoring:[36] This is a critical step in qualitative risk analysis. Probability and impact scoring criteria are listed in the Risk Management Plan. Your scoring system needs to be approved by all stakeholders. Setting a pre-determined scoring system can be included in your Organizational Process Assets as a type of Probability and Impact Matrix.

- It is important to clearly define the probability and impact criteria in your Risk Management Plan. For instance, if you are scoring probability on a scale of 1 to5, you need to detail which factors would comprise a score of 4. This will help remove bias and will improve how you analyze risks.

> If James identified a risk for a 12-month project with a probability of 20%, it would remain that way if no new information was added or if the scores were not altered. In this way, when the project reaches month 7 and probability needs to be recalculated, the score will remain the same. Do not overanalyze scores if no new data has impacted the results.

---

36   PMP Exam Tip: Why Do We Use a Probability and Impact Matrix?, https://www.project-management-prepcast.com/index.php/freetry-it/free-pmp-tips/pmp-exam-tips/315-pmp-exam-tip-why-do-we-use-a-probability-and-impact-matrix

- Bias: Motivational and cognitive types of bias do need to be removed from scoring by defining them early on. Try to find unbiased sources to help score risks in order to make them as accurate as possible. Qualitative Risk Analysis needs accurate and unbiased data if it is going to be applicable in your strategy.

- Frequency: Perform Qualitative Risk Analysis is an iterative process. For this purpose, establish defined guidelines in your Risk Management Plan. Qualitative Risk Analysis is quick and needs to be done every time a new risk is identified.

- Urgency: Your urgency levels need to be defined, documented, and confirmed by your team and stakeholders. Build a probability and impact matrix that will allow prioritization based on score. Your company might have a standard matrix that they use, in which case it should be in your Organizational Process Assets. If not, you will have to create one yourself. Here is an example of a simple matrix.

Low Priority Score	Moderate Priority Score	High Priority Score
8 or below	9–12	13–25

- Quality Data: While qualitative risk analysis is purely subjective, you must, however, make sure that your data is accurate. That means guaranteeing that your probability and impact scoring data and decisions are reliable.

Actively Performing These Functions

With complex and ambitious projects, it makes sense to institute a stringent risk analysis process. Qualitative risk analysis[37] is first and foremost the process of prioritizing risk. Once you understand that, you can use any number of tools to help you focus your time and effort on the right high-priority risks.

- Probability: A risk that may occur
- Impact: The effect a risk has on the project

Below is another basic form for creating a Risk Impact and Probability model/matrix.

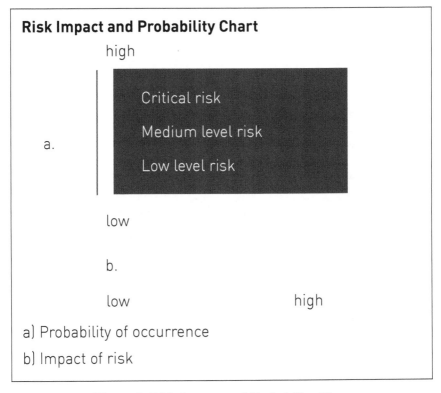

Figure 2: Risk Impact and Probability Chart

37   Risk Impact and Probability Chart, http://www.mindtools.com/pages/article/newPPM_78.htm

- *Low impact/low probability*: The bottom of the chart reflects low level risks, which can be ignored as they are acceptable risks within your predefined plan.
- *Low impact/high probability*: If your risks fall at the top left, they are of moderate importance. You may or may not have a response prepared, but you should attempt to reduce the chance of them occurring.
- *High impact/high probability*: Risks at the top right corner are of critical importance and can cause serious damage if they occur. These are your very top priority risks for which you must create responses.
- *High impact/low probability*: Risks at the bottom right corner are of high importance and need to be monitored, although they are unlikely to happen. These must have prepared responses for eventualities to keep the project on track—that means contingency plans need to be ready and waiting for action.

Project managers have the ability to build their own models depending on their comfort level, expertise, and preferences. It is key that you understand this so that you can work within multiple models if the need arises.

Contextualizing Qualitative Risk Analysis

Before we continue, it makes sense to speak about Qualitative Risk Analysis in context. Because much of qualitative research is social-based, there are many forms of analysis that are not done often enough.

For example, a qualitative interview done for a recent project is unlikely to be reanalyzed for a new project. The risk owner occasionally impedes the reuse of data, which can be problematic for you. While secondary analysis is not usually required, it can be desperately needed in specific areas.

That is why it is important to understand that minimal threat actually exists with decontextualization[38]—and that there is more benefit to secondary analysis than previously believed. Project managers have always resisted sharing qualitative data for this reason; they fear that results will change or subjective opinions will be called into question.

But when you look at qualitative risk analysis as a group function and share openly with your project team, there is no need to prevent the sharing of qualitative data in any context. It is useful when utilized in similar projects and can only benefit from multiple perspectives, especially if those perspectives are of experienced stakeholders.

Collaborative reanalysis of qualitative data can be extremely useful, and because it is so important for this data to be accurate and non-biased, it stands to reason that placing it in context— that is, understanding the needs from multiple perspectives— will greatly improve your ability to manage risks overall as it fuels your strategic processes.

In context, all qualitative analysis should be exposed to many rounds of analysis by anyone who is interested in improving the process. Old beliefs that secondary analysis only pertains to quantitative data need to be reformed. Your risk scoring methods need to be on target, and the only way you are going to achieve this is if you are open to secondary analysis.

Another way of working with context in qualitative analysis is when you discover a new risk. When this happens, you need to reanalyze your Qualitative Risk data so that it is seamlessly integrated, updated, and correct. At this stage, there is an opportunity for improvement, so if you expose the data to

---

38   Harry Van Den Berg, Reanalyzing Qualitative Interviews From Different Angles: The Risk of Decontextualization and Other Problems of Sharing Qualitative Data, http://www.qualitative-research.net/index.php/fqs/article/view/499/1074

secondary analysis by a new stakeholder or new members of your team, it will provide you with additional insights and opinions.

Getting into the habit of sharing your qualitative data and actively seeking out new perspectives for improvement will strengthen your strategy. This is the new context in which project managers should be working, leaving the old assumptions about secondary analysis behind because they are no longer threatening.

Study Success: 5 Sample Questions

Based on the information you have learned about Qualitative Risk Analysis, answer the following questions.

1. *Name the seven outputs that you can expect to find in your Risk Register after completing Perform Qualitative Risk Analysis.*

2. *Explain what a Risk Rating is and why it is needed.*

3. *Outline how to calculate Risk Exposure.*

4. *When is the most important time to use Qualitative Risk Analysis?*

5. *How can secondary analysis be useful in Qualitative Risk Analysis?*

Answers:

Answer 1: Risk Ratings, Project Risk Score, Category Grouping, Urgent List, Additional Analysis, Watch Lists, and Risk Trends

Answer 2: Ranking or prioritizing risk is done by adding Risk Ratings to your Risk Register. All risks should be added this way so that each risk probability and impact is assigned a Risk Rating. Do not forget to multiply the probability and impact Risk Ratings to achieve your Risk Score and Risk Exposure.

Answer 3: Probability × Impact Risk Ratings = Risk Score, then Total Amount of Combined Risk Scores = Project Risk Score and Project Risk Scores = Risk Exposure Calculation

Answer 4: After Plan Risk Management and Risk Identification—and when a new risk is discovered during the project once analysis is "over."

Answer 5: To incorporate multiple perspectives to strengthen your ongoing Project Risk Management Plan at the Qualitative data level so that your scoring results are more accurate and multi-faceted

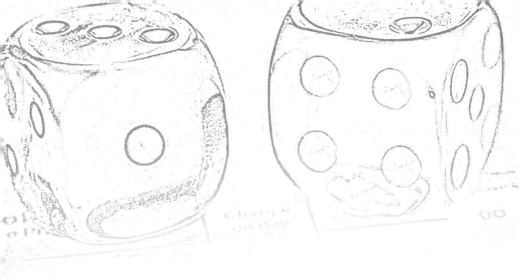

CHAPTER 8

PERFORM QUANTITATIVE RISK ANALYSIS -PART I

"You can use all the quantitative data you can get, but you still have to distrust it and use your own intelligence and judgment."

ALVIN TOFFLER

PIER-C: Following Qualitative Analysis, your next step is to Perform Quantitative Risk Analysis. This is an optional step for project risk managers in some organizations. The project team's decision about whether or not you need to perform this type of analysis will be based on a number of external factors, such as project complexity and priority, time, effort, and benefit comparisons.

When you use this kind of evaluation method, you are working with numerical, or numbers-based, analysis that will help you determine the impact that multiple risks might have on your project. Unlike Qualitative Analysis, which is subjective (influenced by personal feelings and experience), Quantitative Analysis is objective (fact based and impartial).

This objective method of analysis helps the project team determine the probability that your outlined budget and schedule outcomes are viable and can be achieved. Again, the Risk Register is updated and refreshed as the end goal of this step.

What Is Quantitative Risk Analysis?

Perform Quantitative Risk Analysis is the fourth step in the Risk Management process, and it is based on complex numerical analysis for greater accuracy in the analysis arena. It uses the updated Risk Register from your Perform Qualitative Risk Analysis segment to add objective risk factor analysis to the findings in your project.

Defined, a quantitative risk analysis[39] is the process for numerically analyzing the effect of overall project objectives of identified risks. It is performed after the qualitative risk analysis once the risks have been prioritized. Then the risks are analyzed, and the effect of those risks is assigned a numerical rating for greater accuracy.

The PMBOK Guide specifically outlines the objectives of Quantitative Risk Analysis. The first is that it quantifies possible project outcomes and probabilities because it simultaneously considers the impact of multiple risks on specific project objectives and outcomes. This activity alone analyzes the effects of risk that could impact your project's competing demands.

Quantitative Risk Analysis also analyzes three key scenarios using the Three-Point Estimating method: *pessimistic, most-likely,* and *optimistic.* Having the ability to assess the probability of achieving your project objectives will improve your strategy.

Many tools are used in this process, one of which is Monte Carlo—a simulation and modeling technique that provides specific timeframes or points at which your risk potential is very high. Standard Deviation Analysis tools are also used; these are effective for measuring the level of dispersion in the data being analyzed.

When you complete Quantitative Risk Analysis, you will be able to successfully identify risks that require your attention by quantifying their relative contribution to your entire project risk. You will also be able to determine real and achievable costs, schedules, scope, and quality targets based on the set of identified risks.

---

39   Quantitative Risk Analysis, http://www.mypmps.net/en/mypmps/ knowledgeareas/risk/quantitative-risk-analysis.html

How to Perform Quantitative Risk Analysis

When you perform quantitative risk analysis, you will be able to arrive at the best project management decisions, especially when certain outcomes and conditions are not clear. These decisions will be objective rather than subjective and therefore much more accurate. More importantly perhaps, senior management will find it easier to accept this information.

Be aware that quantitative risk analysis is done infrequently in that it is *not* always conducted as qualitative analysis must be. You need to consider several factors before deciding to launch into a complex and time-consuming quantitative analysis.

- Take project features like cost, length, and priority of the project into account.
- Look at the project complexity, and make a go or no-go decision.
- Examine the amount of time and effort required versus the benefits of in-depth quantitative analysis.

Performing these numerical analyses requires the use of a basic three-structure approach: taking inputs, tools and techniques, and outputs into account.

In the exam, you may be asked to describe the Perform Quantitative Risk Analysis process.

Project Risk Management in Practice!

James and his team have decided to perform a quantitative risk analysis process consisting of inputs, tools and techniques, and outputs.

Inputs	Tools & Techniques	Outputs
• Risk Management Plan • Cost Management Plan • Schedule Management Plan • Risk Register • Enterprise environmental factors • Organizational Process Assets	• Data Gathering and Representation Techniques • Quantitative Risk Analysis and Modeling Techniques • Expert Judgement	• Project documents updates

In the exam, you may be asked to describe the Perform Quantitative Risk Analysis process.

The Quantitative Risk Analysis[40] process numerically analyzes the effect of identified risk events on overall project objectives. It is performed on risks that have been prioritized by the Qualitative Risk Analysis process. These have been cited as potentially and substantially impacting your project's needs. It is not required on all projects and usually depends on time and budget. However, if you have decided to conduct it at the beginning, it must be performed again once your Plan Risk Responses and Control Risks processes have been completed to test for impact and effect.

The Quantitative Risk Analysis Process Explained

Quantitative Risk Analysis follows the Qualitative Risk Analysis process because these are key inputs needed to move ahead with numerical analysis. Many times you cannot conduct an accurate quantitative analysis if your qualitative data is not complete.

Using the desired inputs, the project team will select from a substantial list of tools and techniques for use in converting

---

40   Cram Flashcards, http://www.cram.com/flashcards/pmbok-chapter-11-project-risk-management-1873570

and elaborating on current data. Because this kind of analysis scrutinizes the effect of risks on overall project objectives numerically, selecting which models and tools to use is important, as well as inputting the relevant data.

As the tools and techniques produce numerical data that are used to update project documents, quantitative risk analysis can be used to streamline processes and actions that the project team will take in Plan Risk Responses. Using data gathering and representation techniques and modeling, the team will produce accurate data that will become part of the project's updated Risk Register.

To review: You would use quantitative analysis if you have project factors that remain unclear that are perhaps inflating your risk potential. To reduce this risk and get a better handle on your decisions, numerical equations contextualize data in a way that allows for objective, sound decision-making.

Combine this with your subjective qualitative data and you will have a strong social and numerical basis for project risk management. Keep in mind that qualitative analysis is occasionally enough to produce strong, unbiased decisions, although it does need multiple perspectives.

If James and his team decided to perform quantitative analysis, it was because there were elements in the subjective analysis from qualitative analysis that remained unclear or required further analysis.

Inputs to Consider With Quantitative Risk Analysis

To Perform Quantitative Risk Analysis, you will need to know what inputs are available so that you can reliably ground your numerical data.

James has compiled the following six inputs to use in quantitative risk analysis:

- Risk Management Plan
- Cost Management Plan
- Schedule Management Plan
- Risk Register
- Enterprise Environmental Factors
- Organizational Process Assets

Learn the definition of each to fully understand the process of selecting these inputs for use in achieving the desired outputs.

- ***Risk Management Plan***: The Risk Management plan helps you define the roles, responsibilities, and methods used to evaluate your risks.
- ***Cost Management Plan***: A cost management plan helps set the format and criteria for planning, structuring, estimating, budgeting, and controlling all of your project costs. These controls assist you in establishing an approach to Quantitative Risk Analysis for your budget plan.
- ***Schedule Management Plan***: A schedule management plan helps you set formulas and criteria for developing and controlling your project timelines and schedule. It manages the nature of your schedule and helps you structure an approach to Quantitative Risk Analysis for your schedule plan.
- ***Risk Register***: The Risk Register provides you with the initial list of risks to be evaluated. It is consistently updated during the project risk management process after

being streamlined in the Plan Risk Management, Identify Risks, and Qualitative Risk Analysis sections.

- *Enterprise Environmental Factors*: They provide guidance and context to the risk analysis based on internal and external factors that influence the project's success.
- *Organizational Process Assets*: These documents include historical information, risk databases, lessons learned, templates, and studies from previous projects. They could also include data on Risk Rating rules.

Using these inputs, you will source the correct tools and techniques to use so that information can be converted into decisions and action in the form of valuable outputs for the next process.

Strategies, Tools and Techniques

Quantitative Risk Analysis can be fairly complex, so it makes sense to take some extra time in this area to fully understand the numerical applications of these models. PMI has divided the tool sets into two areas.

- *Data Gathering and Representation Techniques*: Data- gathering techniques primarily consist of interviews, while data representation techniques are comprised of probability distributions. Probability distributions can be made up of continuous, discrete, uniform, beta, or triangular distributions.
- *Quantitative Risk Analysis and Modeling Techniques*: The data gathered from the previous process step is used to perform a host of analysis to determine the impact that certain risks will have on the project as the team works towards meeting the objectives. Analysis using specific models is the most direct route to success here.

James has compiled the following tools and techniques to perform quantitative risk analysis with his team based on their inputs:

- Data Gathering and Representation Techniques
- Interviewing
- Probability Distributions
- Normal Distributions
- Uniform Distributions
- Three Point Estimating
- PERT
- Standard Deviation
- Triangular Distributions
- Beta Distributions
- Quantitative Risk Analysis and Modeling Techniques
- Sensitivity Analysis
- Monte Carlo
- Latin Hypercube Sampling (LHS)
- Tornado Diagram
- Expected Monetary Value
- Decision Tree Analysis
- Expert Judgment

Learn the definition and function of each so that you can make your own selections when you want to perform an in-depth quantitative analysis.

Data Gathering and Representation Techniques

Data gathering and representation techniques are used to collect, organize, and present data and information. They include a number of techniques.

- *Interviewing*: Interviews are the main source of data gathering and closely adhere to the assessment values mentioned above (optimistic, pessimistic, realistic).
- *Probability Distributions*: These distributions show the probability of an event occurring within a specific project.
- *Normal Distributions*: Also known as a Gaussian Distribution, a normal distribution is one in which the data are evenly distributed around the mean. In other words, the normal distribution is symmetric about its mean. Normal or Gaussian distributions are important for probability distribution in statistics. The Gaussian Distribution is also informally referred to as the Bell Curve or the Gaussian Bell Curve.

- *Uniform Distributions*: This is the simplest form of distribution that calculates equal probabilities. This shows scenarios where no single value is more likely to happen than another.
- *Three Point Estimating*: Three Point Estimating Technique uses three values to estimate duration (or cost). These values are usually provided from experts or reliable historical data. The three values are pessimistic (worst case scenario), the most likely estimate, and optimistic (best case scenario). The triangular distribution and weighted average are two common estimating methods under three point estimating. Weighted average is also known as the PERT formula, Estimated Activity Duration (EAD), Beta Distribution, and Estimated Time (T_E).

- **PERT**: Program Evaluation and Review Technique, or PERT, is a statistical tool used in project risk management to analyze and represent the tasks involved in completing any given project.
- **Standard Deviation**: Standard deviation in statistics and probability theory measures the amount of variation or dispersion from the average.
- **Triangular Distributions**: A triangular distribution uses the estimate values based on your three point estimate to quantify risk for each work breakdown structure.
- **Beta Distributions**: A beta distribution is used to describe the uncertainty about the probability of occurrence of an event.

Quantitative Risk Analysis and Modeling Techniques

The PMBOK Guide outlines a few main data gathering and representation techniques that are available for use in quantitative risk analysis:

- **Sensitivity Analysis**: Sensitivity analysis involves analyzing project variables to determine how sensitive the project is to specific risks by analyzing the impact and severity of each of those variables.
- **Monte Carlo**: Monte Carlo analysis involves determining the impact of the project's identified risks by running simulations to identify the range of possible outcomes for a number of scenarios. You might also encounter Latin Hypercube Sampling (LHS) in the exam. Much like Monte Carlo simulation, LHS is also a modeling and simulation technique. While they have different technical and statistical approaches, both Monte Carlo and LHS are unbiased estimation techniques.

- *Tornado Diagram*: A funnel-shaped diagram used to portray project sensitivity to cost and other factors, it represents the impact of risks for specific aspects or variables.

- *Expected Monetary Value*: To determine the expected monetary value for a risk, multiply the likelihood by the cost impact to get an expected value for each risk. Add these together to get the expected monetary value for the project.

- *Decision Tree Analysis*: A decision tree analysis is a flow diagram in which each rectangle contains a description of the risk and its cost. These are linked with arrows, each of which leads to another box that represents percentage probability. Totals are calculated by multiplying risk cost by probability and adding that value to the initial cost.

Become familiar with these basic concepts before we go into their details in the next chapter. You will be able to see what they look like and how they work, but first you need to be familiar with their definitions.

Study Success: 5 Sample Questions

Based on the information you have learned about Perform Quantitative Risk Analysis, answer the following questions.

1. *Choose the most accurate answer in the following multiple choice questions.*

    a. Describe the process of Perform Quantitative Risk Analysis.

    b. Numerical analysis that looks at the effect of identified risk on project objectives

    c. Numerical analysis that looks at the impact of Plan Risk Responses

    d. Social analysis that looks at the impact of overall project risk objectives

    e. Numerical analysis that looks at cost, schedule, and projected outcomes

2. *Name three Inputs for Perform Quantitative Risk Analysis.*

    a. Risk Register, Decision Tree, Risk Management Plan

    b. Organization Process Assets, Risk Register, Cost Management Plan

    c. Risk Management Plan, Risk Register, Monte Carlo Analysis

    d. Organizational Process Assets, Probability Distributions, Cost Management Plan

3. *Which order makes the most sense in terms of the Quantitative Risk Analysis process?*

   a. Interviews, Decision Trees, Monte Carlo Analysis, Risk Data Quality Assessment

   b. Risk Probability and Impact Assessment, Data Gathering, PERT

   c. Three Point Estimating, Interviews, Risk Analysis, Standard Deviation

   d. Qualitative Data, Interviews, Probability Distributions, Decision Trees

4. *Define a probability distribution.*

   a. Shows the probability of risk occurring within a broad range of models

   b. Shows the probability of an event occurring within a specific timeline and budget

   c. Shows the probability of an event occurring within a specific project

   d. Shows the probability of risk occurring in Quantitative Risk Analysis

5. *What is a Tornado Diagram?*

   a. A funnel-shaped diagram that shows project sensitivity to cost and other factors

   b. A tornado-shaped diagram that runs simulations to identify the range of possible outcomes for a number of scenarios

   c. A funnel-shaped diagram that analyzes the severity of each risk in your project

   d. A tornado-shaped diagram that multiplies risk and projects specific outputs

Answers:

Answer 1: A

Answer 2: B

Answer 3: D

Answer 4: C

Answer 5: A

CHAPTER 9

PERFORM QUANTITATIVE RISK ANALYSIS-PART II

"We have no future because our present is too volatile. We have only risk management."

WILLIAM GIBSON

This is the second part of the Perform Quantitative Risk Analysis section and goes into greater detail about the two kinds of Quantitative Risk Analysis that can be performed to help you make more informed decisions about project risks.

This section will also cover the outputs for Perform Quantitative Risk Analysis and highlight important facts for your project team to remember when working through this stage as a project risk manager.

Representation and Data Gathering Processes

The first step in this evaluation process is to gather the relevant data that you will be using. You cannot move on if you have not first completed the initial data gathering.

Data Gathering and Representation Techniques

Interviewing: As the central and most important element in data gathering, interviewing stakeholders is required to determine risk impact. These interviews are often used to determine the three scenarios (optimistic, pessimistic, and most-likely) for time and cost estimates.

These subjective estimates are then used when you have selected a Three Point Estimating method like PERT. It is important to include a blend of open-ended and prepared questions when these interviews are conducted. Open-ended questions help you gain insight from the person being interviewed, after which you can continue with specific, predetermined questions.

It is useful to note that at this stage, executing Quantitative Risk Analysis is a lengthy process. If there are multiple stakeholders, interviews can involve several iterations.

Three Point Estimating and PERT

Three point estimating uses the optimistic, most-likely, and pessimistic values provided by your interviewed experts or stakeholders to determine the best possible estimates.

Take a look at this example:

Estimate to Complete Activity	Number of Days Estimated
Optimistic	5 days
Most Likely	10 days
Pessimistic	21 days

- Three Point Averaging using Triangular Distribution: Three point averaging takes the three estimates and averages them to find the best possible estimate. To use the example above, simply apply the formula. Add the numbers above together; then divide them by 3 to determine the average.

  Step 1: 5 + 10 + 21 = 36

  Step 2: 36/3 = 12

  Therefore, your best estimate = 12 days. This is the method used in your test if the question refers to triangular distribution.

- PERT: This stands for Program Evaluation and Review

Technique. This second part of three point estimating involves finding a weighted average using PERT. That means that PERT assumes that all results fall within a standard deviation. The formula for calculating a PERT estimate is:

PERT

Pessimistic + (4 × Most Likely) + Optimistic

6

Calculate by substantiating the values in the example:

(21 + (4 × 10) + 5) = 66/6 = 11 days for the estimate

6

Standard Deviation: A standard deviation is calculated using optimistic, pessimistic, and most-likely values. Like the two previous formulas, there is an equation used to determine standard deviation:

STANDARD DEVIATION

Pessimistic − Optimistic

6

Calculate by substantiating the values in the example:

21 days − 5 days = 16/6 = 2.67 standard deviation

6

If you are asked to calculate variance, it is done by squaring your standard deviation figure. If standard deviation is 3, then your variance will be 3 times 3, which equals 9.

All in all, Three Point Estimation is simple if you remember the formulas:

- Triangular Distribution: Add the estimates; then average them.
- Weighted Average:
$$\frac{Pessimistic + (4 \times Most\ Likely) + Optimistic}{6}$$
- Standard Deviation: $\dfrac{Pessimistic - Optimistic}{6}$
- Variance = standard deviation squared

Probability Distributions: In context, a probability distribution estimates the potential of a risk event happening over a pre-described range of time. Because of this, there are a number of distribution types that you could use that will impact risk management analysis success.

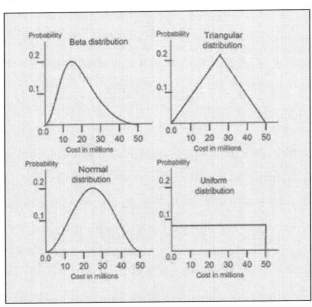

Figure 3: Types of Probability Distribution41

---

41   Probability Distributions, http://getpmpcertified.blogspot.com/2011_06_01_archive.html

Normal Distributions: A normal distribution is estimated using the Three Point method to create the normal distribution. The curve here is referred to as a bell curve. This kind of model uses averages and Sigma intervals to reflect the potential range of values along the length of the curve on the graph. You can see the bell curve in the graphic below; the vertical line at the center is the mean (average), and the vertical lines on either side of it are the Sigma intervals.

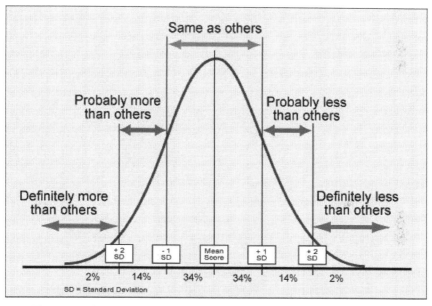

Figure 4 : A performance assessment using a normal distribution[42]

Generally, the higher the standard deviation, the greater the risk will be. A Standard Deviation is a numeric indicator that will help you calculate the range of potential results. It represents the distance you travel from the mean (average, vertical line) as you reach across the normal distribution.

---

42   Derek Huether, Performance Assessment and Drinking Kool-Aid, http://thecriticalpath.info/tag/bell-curve/

When the range is great, so is the risk. For example, if your mean is 20, you can see how the range alters when you compare a standard deviation of 2 with one of 3.

- **1 Sigma:** results occur 4 out of 6 times
- **2 and 3 Sigma:** results occur 1 out of 6 times

Looking at the following graphs, the percentage of returns that fall within each Sigma range in the normal distribution or bell curve is:

- **1 Sigma:** Results occur within the 1 Sigma range 68.26% of the time. When you estimate this, you can assume returns fall within 1 Sigma of the mean four out of six times. Using a standard deviation of 2, the results range from 18 to 22 at 1 Sigma. When the standard deviation becomes 3, this increases from 17 to 23 in Sigma 1. A greater range means greater risk overall.
- **2 Sigma:** Here results happen within 2 Sigma 95.46% of the time. You can see a standard deviation of 2 is 16–24 at 2 Sigma. When you increase it to 3, the 2 Sigma range moves from 14 to 26. Again, risk increases when the standard deviation increases.
- **3 Sigma:** Here results occur within 3 Sigma 99.73% of the time. You can assume returns fall within 2 and 3 Sigma range on each side of the mean 1 out of 6 times. Results from standard deviation of 2 will range from 14 to 26 at 3 Sigma. But the range increases from 11 to 29 when the standard deviation is 3—meaning more risk is incurred.

For test-taking purposes, remember that 6 Sigma = 99.99985% or not more than 3.4 defects per million opportunities (DPMO).

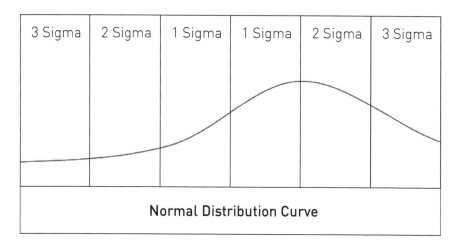

3 Sigma	2 Sigma	1 Sigma	1 Sigma	2 Sigma	3 Sigma

Normal Distribution Curve

Optimistic			Most Likely	Pessimistic		
Sigma 3	Sigma 2	Sigma 1	Mean	Sigma 1	Sigma 2	Sigma 3
14	16	18	20 (SD=2)	22	24	26
11	14	17	20 (SD=3)	23	26	29

Uniform Distributions: These are used in Perform Quantitative Risk Analysis as another form of distribution. Risk here is commonly uniform in the early design stages of the project, and only becomes non-uniform later on.

- All cost values within uniform distribution have the same probability of being achieved. The f axis is probability; the X axis is cost.

Triangular Distributions: These illustrate where your probability peaks at the mean. There is a quick decrease in probability as results move away from the mean.

Probability peaks in the middle. The f axis denotes probability, the X axis cost.

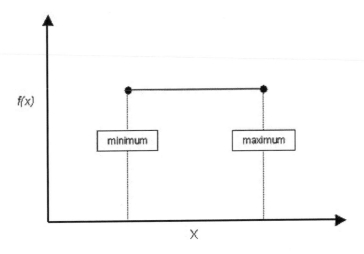

Figure 5 : A Uniform Distribution Model[43]

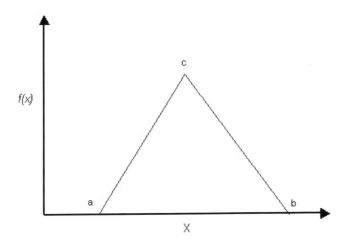

Figure 6: A Triangular Distribution44

Beta Distributions: Indicate probability peaks on either side of the mean

---

43 Uniform Distribution, https://www.rocscience.com/help/swedge/webhelp/swedge/Uniform_Distribution.htm

44 Triangular Distribution, https://www.rocscience.com/help/swedge/webhelp/swedge/Triangular_Distribution.htm

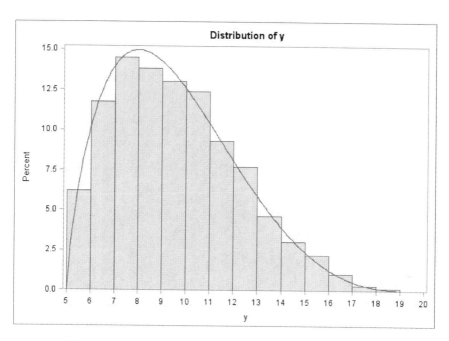

Figure 7 : A Beta distribution showing a left-side peak[45]

Here is an example of two distributions on the same graph (normal and beta):

---

45   Rick Wicklin, That Distribution Is Quite PERT!, http://blogs.sas.com/content/iml/2012/10/24/pert-distribution/

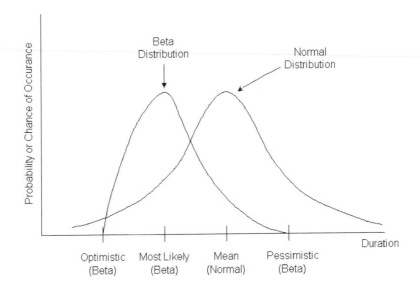

Figure 8: Two distributions on the same graph (normal and beta)

Quantitative Risk Modeling Techniques

Once you have established your estimates and converted your subjective data into numerical values, you can continue to the next step, which uses Quantitative Risk Modeling techniques. These are excellent for use in a variety of estimates and determinations.

Quantitative Risk Analysis and Modeling Techniques

Sensitivity Analysis: A sensitivity analysis uses several "what if" scenarios to help you calculate your potential results. This is a modeling technique that will assist you in determining which risks would have the greatest impact on your project.

- Sensitivity analysis and "What If" Scenario Analysis both can use Monte Carlo as the technique for determining these factors.
- Monte Carlo: A Monte Carlo traditionally uses optimistic,

most-likely, and pessimistic estimates to determine the probability of meeting cost and schedule goals. The results of data gathering and representation techniques are often recorded using a variety of different modeling techniques. A typical model that shows project potential to satisfy certain organizational cost objectives looks like this:

- **Tornado Diagram:** A tornado diagram is the result of a Sensitivity Analysis. It shows a single factor like the Net Present Value or Average Game Profitability and then displays the variables and their level of sensitivity or impact to the project. For example:

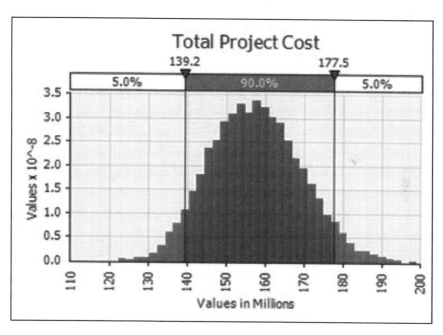

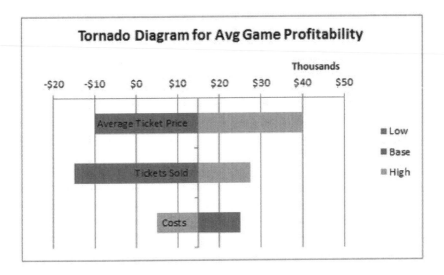

Figure 9: A Tornado Diagram[46]

- ***Expected Monetary Value (EMV):*** A method commonly used to establish Contingency Reserve requirements for your budget and schedule. EMV is an estimate quantified by multiplying probability times the best or worst case (cost or time) scenario. This will give you the best "expected monetary value" in risk. EMV takes the anti-value of negative risk into account.

Imagine that James encountered four risks that impacted his product launch, and he marked them A, B, C, and D.

- Risk A has been found to have a 30% chance of happening, and if it does, it will cost his project $40,000 as a negative risk. James's job is to calculate the required Contingency Reserves for this risk using EMV. The calculation is then .3 × $40,000 = $12,000, which is added to the project budget.

---

46   Tornado Diagram, http://en.wikipedia.org/wiki/Tornado_diagram

- Risk B has been found to have a 40% chance of happening but will save the project ($10,000). Amounts in parenthesis save your project money and need to be subtracted from your overall contingency reserve amounts. This risk is positive, so your calculation would be .4 × $10,000 = $4000. Subtract that from your budget.
- Risk C has 75% chance of happening and will cost the project $60,000 as a negative risk. Again, James uses EMV to calculate the amount (.75 × $60,000 = $45,000).
- Risk D has a 50% chance of happening and will cost the project $30,000 (.5 × $30,000 = $15,000).

To calculate the overall Contingency Reserves required for the project, you need to add all of the negative risks and subtract the positive risks. Here is an example:

Risk	Probability	Maximum Dollar Impact of Risk	Contingency Money Requirements
A	30%	$40,000	$12,000
B	40%	($10,000)	($4000.00)
C	75%	$60,000	$45,000
D	50%	$30,000	$15,000
Total	Add $68,000 to project budget for contingency reserve needs.		$68,000

As a variation of this, if Risk D does actually happen, the Contingency Reserves will use $30,000, leaving $38,000 remaining in contingency funds. However, the project will not be impeded by a lack of financial coverage.

Decision Tree Analysis: A decision tree analysis outlines a scenario under consideration and uses the data to determine the most economical approach. The core goal of a decision tree analysis is to select the scenario that has the best overall Expected Monetary Value, or EMV. This is the highest EMV return or lowest EMV cost. It is the most effective tool for the development of appropriate risk responses.

Here are some EMV scenarios to help you better understand the concept:

- *Return + Return*: James has a project with a fixed return of $100,000. There is a 20% chance of additional returns of $50,000 if the project finishes ahead of schedule. The value here will be calculated as:

  $0.2 \times \$50,000 = 10,000$
  $\$100,000 + \$10,000 = \$110,000$

- *Cost + Cost:* James has a project with a set cost of $60,000. There is a 60% chance of incurring additional costs of $40,000 due to delays. The total cost estimate is:

  $\$60,000 + (.6 \times \$40,000) = \$60,000 + \$24,000 = \$84,000$

- *Return − Cost*: James has a project with a guaranteed return of $200,000. There is a 40% chance that the returns will be reduced by $80,000 because of overrunning costs. The revised return projection is therefore:

  $(\$200,00 - (.4 \times \$80,000)) = (\$200,000 - \$32,000) = \$168,000$

On the exam, you may be presented with two scenarios; try to select the option with the lowest cost and highest returns. If you are shown a decision tree diagram, you will have to analyze the scenarios there. Choose the option with the highest return, lowest cost.

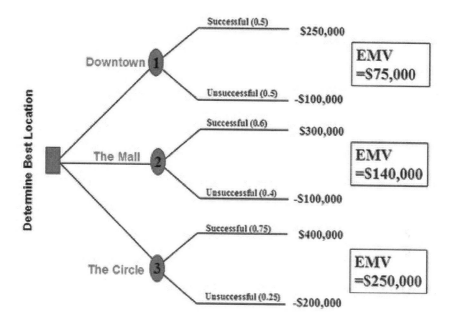

Figure 10: Decision tree diagram

Outputs Involved in Quantitative Risk Analysis

When you have completed your Quantitative Risk Analysis, you will need to update the Risk Register once again. At that point, you will have clearly defined probabilities of meeting defined costs and specific schedule objectives.

- *Updating the Risk Register*: Always make sure that you update your Risk Register, which means updating your probability and impact of the risks that will influence your project goals. These can be either positive or negative.

- *Probabilistic Analysis*: A probabilistic analysis of a project asks what the potential time and cost outcomes will be based on mathematical criteria and analysis.

> James has compiled the following project document updates as outputs resulting from quantitative risk analysis:
>
> - Updating the Risk Register
> - Probabilistic Analysis
> - Probability of achieving cost and time objectives
> - Prioritized List of Quantified Risks
> - Trends in Quantified Risk Analysis
>
> Learn the definition of each to fully understand the process of achieving these outputs by correctly selecting inputs and tools and techniques and using them to inform your outcome.

- ***Probability of Achieving Cost and Time Objectives***: This type of quantitative risk analysis lets you factor risk into your budget and schedule estimates. This adjusted data will be compared against original time and cost estimations.
- ***Prioritized List of Quantified Risks***: Ask which risks are more likely to happen based on your new numeric results.
- ***Trends in Quantified Risk Analysis***: This focuses on a trend of mathematical outcomes, which can be determined if your impact of risk decreases or increases as your project progresses.

Based on your results from the quantitative risk analysis, you will update your Risk Register. For an example, see the graph below:

Risk	Cause	Risk Owner	Category	Risk Response	Probability Risk Rating	Impact Risk Rating	Risk Score
		Initial		Initial	Update in step 4	Update in step 4	Update in step 4
					Update in step 4	Update in step 4	Update in step 4

Update your Risk Register at the end of your perform quantitative risk analysis phase.

The Quantitative Risk Analysis Success Roadmap

Focus on these key success points if you want to excel at Quantitative Risk Analysis. These points will help you perform the functions in this section with greater ease and accuracy.

- *Quality Data*: With quantitative risk analysis being an objective function, you must make sure that data sources are unbiased and accurate. You need to use tools such as interviewing to get the additional expert insight you need to begin your analysis.
- *Quality Modeling*: This kind of analysis requires the use of models for effective outcomes. Choose the model that best supports your project needs—like decision trees, cost estimates, and project schedules.
- *Perform Qualitative Risk Analysis*: It is recommended to perform qualitative risk analysis before the project team launches into quantitative risk analysis. The highest priority risks should be evaluated at this stage to determine their impact on your project. Initial risk prioritization is provided at the qualitative stage.

- *Repeating*: To assess benefits of risk responses, a key best practice here is to conduct quantitative risk analysis at the end of plan risk responses; if you previously completed this analysis in a similar project, you may reuse the data but must be certain that the figures are still accurate.
- *Relationships:* Focus on spotting relationships that lie between multiple risks. Begin to understand how one risk impacts and leads to other types of risks.
- *Bias*: Reduce cognitive and motivational bias in your social data to improve the accuracy of your estimates.

Qualitative vs. Quantitative Risk Analysis

To better understand the difference between qualitative and quantitative risk analysis, here is a comparison chart that outlines those differences.

Perform Qualitative Risk Analysis	Perform Quantitative Risk Analysis
Subjective	Objective
Always accomplished	Only done when value is present and the process is worth the time and effort
Fast	Takes time and expertise
Addresses individual risk	Predicts likely outcomes based on the review of multiple risk factors.
Scores risk using probability × impact	Uses numerical analysis like probability distribution, EMV and decision trees to assess risk
Output is prioritized list of risks	Output is the probability of meeting defined project outcomes.
Prioritizes individual risk	Identifies risks with greatest impact to project objectives
Risk register is updated at the conclusion of these activities.	

Study Success: 5 Sample Questions

Based on the information you have learned about Plan Risk Responses, answer the following questions.

1. *Which three scenarios/values are used to determine cost and schedule estimates in Quantitative Risk Analysis?*
   a. Three point estimating, three point averaging, standard deviation
   b. Quantitative data, qualitative data, PERT
   c. Optimistic, pessimistic, and most likely values
   d. Estimations, calculations, risks

2. *Define the function of Three Point Averaging.*
   a. It uses a three point method to create a normal distribution graph.
   b. It uses a weighted average and PERT to determine the estimates.
   c. It adds the estimates together then squares them to determine accuracy.
   d. It takes three estimates and averages them to find the best estimate.

3. *Name three types of distribution.*
   a. Normal distribution, uniform distribution, triangular distribution
   b. Normal distribution, unbiased distribution, beta distribution
   c. Normal distribution, triangular distribution, estimate distribution
   d. Normal distribution, probability distribution, uniform distribution

4. What does a tornado diagram do?

a. After a Monte Carlo, it determines which risks have the greatest impact on your campaign.

b. After a sensitivity analysis, it displays a single factor and multiple surrounding factors.

c. Before an Expected Monetary Value, it is used to quantify multiple probabilities.

d. After a contingency reserve, it determines the cost required for each risk.

5. Calculate the EMV if James has a fixed project cost of $200,000 and there is a 40% chance of additional costs of $20,000.

a. ($8000 + (.4 × $20,000)) = ($200,000 + $20,000) = $220,000

b. ($200,00 + (.4 × $20,000)) = ($200,000 + $8000) = $208,000

c. ($200,00 + (.8 × $40,000)) = ($200,000 + $8000) = $208,000

d. ($200,00 + (.4 × $20,000)) = ($200,000 + $28000) = $228,000

Answers:

Answer 1: C

Answer 2: D

Answer 3: A

Answer 4: B

Answer 5: B

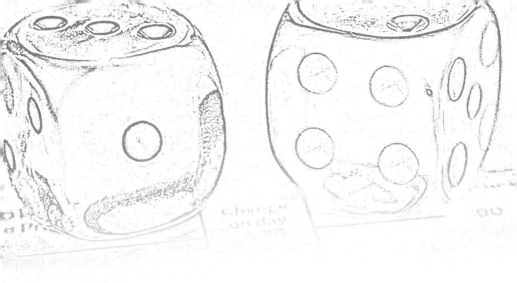

CHAPTER 10
PLAN RISK RESPONSES

"All courses of action are risky, so prudence is not in avoiding danger (it's impossible) but calculating risk and acting decisively. Make mistakes of ambition and not mistakes of sloth. Develop the strength to do bold things, not the strength to suffer."

NICCOLO MACHIAVELLI, THE PRINCE

$\mathbf{P}$IER-C: The next process of the Risk Management arena is Plan Risk Responses, in which the project team develops responses to the risks identified and analyzed so far. The project team will determine the level of response based on the priority and severity of risks. Look for responses that deal with both positive and negative risks.

Positive risks are opportunities, while negative risks are threats; you should respond accordingly. Your Risk Register will be updated at the end of this stage. In addition, a contractual agreement may be developed to support your response strategies that need the involvement of third parties. One way of dealing with negative risk is to transfer it to a third party.

What Is Plan Risk Response?

Defined, Plan Risk Response is the fifth step in your Risk Management Process. Your main goals are to validate your risk responses and the risk owners that have been identified during your Identify Risks process. You also need to develop responses for your urgent list risks and assign new risk owners as you see fit.

To correctly address risks in this section, there are seven distinct risk responses that have been outlined to assist you, three working with negative risk and three for positive risk. The final response is used for both negative and positive risks. Each response will be outlined in the tools and techniques section.

Understand the following terms:

- *Risk Owner*: A risk owner is someone that is assigned a risk and a plan risk response during the project. Confirmed ownership is required. These risk owners formulate responses and monitor the status of their risk while implementing contingency plans and even fallback plans as required. Any stakeholder in your project can be a risk owner. Risk owners are best utilized during the Plan Risk Response and Monitor and Control Risk stages.

- *Risk Action Owner*: This is someone that is assigned to a specific risk by the risk owner in order to help implement the approved risk responses.

- *Contingency Plans and Risk Response:* These are the main responses to any risk. In complex projects, you can develop a fallback plan as well, which is a secondary plan that backs up your contingency plan should it fail.

- *Residual Risks*: These are risks that remain once your Risk Response Plan or Contingency Plan take effect. If a response addresses 80% of risk impact, the remaining 20% would be the residual risk. You should create contingency plans and fallback plans to respond to residual risks of which you are aware. A risk audit could uncover new residual risks, in which case you should log the risk in the risk register and then perform qualitative risk analysis.

- *Secondary Risk*: This is the risk that results from a risk response. The risk register also has a place for secondary risks. An example would be hiring a vendor for project work, which may or may not lead to vendor management risks. These would be clearly documented as secondary risks and should never have a higher risk rating than that of the primary risk from which it came from.

Go/no-go decisions may result from Plan Risk Responses. A no-go decision is made when critical risks do not yet have a response or if the project risk score is above certain thresholds and the situation could not be addressed correctly.

The level of detail defined in risk response needs to be based on the priority of risks. High priority risks require greater levels of detail than lower priority risks.

Risk responses may cause the schedule baseline and cost performance baseline to change, which will require additional work. You will have to get approval for this risk response from an available project sponsor.

- The Risk Register should contain all identified risks. Responses are promptly developed for risks that are on the Urgent List first.

- Risk owners are initially identified during the Identify Risks stage. They are confirmed in the Plan Risk Responses process.

- Risk owners help monitor all risks to which they are assigned. They will periodically create status updates and will respond to their risks as necessary. They can also assign risk action owners if they need additional help with responses.

- Risk Response Plans and contingency risks are developed by risk owners. These owners also identify potential triggers, which are events that provide early warning that a risk is about to happen. When a trigger or warning sign arises, the risk response plan is put into action.

- Fallback plans are also developed by your risk owner, and these are only implemented if your contingency plan does not have the desired response.

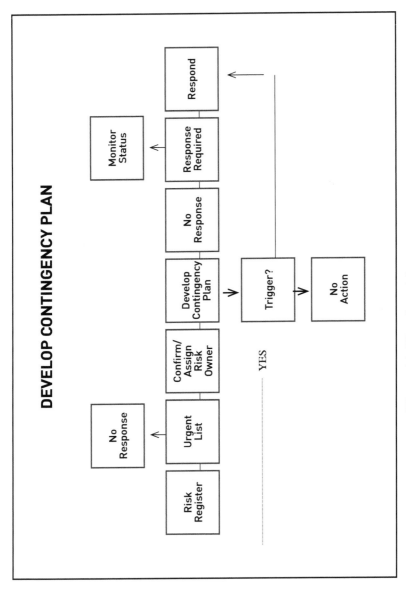

Figure 11: The plan risk response process

The Process of Plan Risk Responses

Like the other processes of Project Risk Management, Plan Risk Responses must focus on certain inputs, tools and techniques, and outputs to be successful.

Project Risk Management in Practice!

James and his team have outlined Plan Risk Responses so that it is easier to work with as they move ahead.

Inputs	Tools & Techniques	Outputs
• Risk Management Plan • Risk Register	• Strategies for Negative Risks or Threats • Strategies for Positive Risks or Opportunities • Contingent Response Strategies • Expert Judgement	• Project documents updates

To succeed with your Plan Risk Response Process, keep the following in mind:

- *Documentation Updates*: Make sure that your agreed on responses are worked into your Project Management Plan. That means technical documentation must be updated as you gain new information from risk responses.
- *Project Manager Support*: While the risk owner is responsible for implementing contingency plans, you, as the project manager, need to get involved when they need support.

- **People**: Ensure that your risk responses are properly communicated with project stakeholders so that they understand their unique roles and responsibilities with risks.
- **Consistency**: Make sure that your responses are aligned with project objectives, stakeholder expectations, and your organizational values. Your responses need to be technically viable to be achieved.
- **Planning**: Your priority of risks will determine the details required in your risk responses. Make sure that key criteria are addressed, such as schedule implications, budget impact, timing, and resource allocations. Your risk owners and risk action owners should develop, manage, and implement your responses to that risk.
- **Analyses**: The link between your risks and risk responses need to be clear, so get agreement or buy-in from your stakeholders for all applicable responses.
- **Opportunities and Threats**: Opportunities are positive risk, and threats are negative risk.

Inputs to Consider With Plan Risk Responses

In Plan Risk Responses, only two inputs are needed. These are both outputs from the previous steps you have carried out with your Risk Management Plan and Risk Register.

James has identified the following two core inputs to use in Plan Risk Responses:

- Risk Management Plan
- Risk Register

Learn the definition of each to fully understand the inputs that drive Plan Risk Responses.

- **Risk Management Plan:** This plan helps define the roles, responsibilities, and methods used to evaluate project risks.
- **Risk Register:** The Risk Register provides the project team with an initial list of risks to evaluate. The Risk Register will be updated during this stage.

Strategies, Tools and Techniques

To Plan Risk Responses, the project team needs a set of tools and techniques to produce the desired outputs. This section focuses on the definitions of these tools and techniques.

James has compiled the following tools and techniques to perform Plan Risk Response with his team:

- Strategies for Negative Risks or Threats
- Strategies for Positive Risks or Opportunities
- Contingent Response Strategies
- Expert Judgment

Learn the definition and function of each so that you can make your own selections when you want to perform Plan Risk Responses using these tools and techniques.

Strategies for Negative Risks and Threats

There are four key strategies for negative risk management:

- *Transference:* This occurs when the response transfers accountability and responsibility to a third party, who performs the work or accepts accountability for the outcome of that work. Normally, there is a cost for transference. Purchasing insurance is an example of transference.

- *Avoidance*: The central focus of avoidance strategy is to remove the cause of the risk. It typically involves modifying the project management plan to eliminate the threat.

- *Mitigation*:This type of response acts to reduce the probability of a risk from happening or—if the risk happens—to reduce its impact. Creating a plan B is mitigation. A good example is training employees so that the risk of poor performance is reduced through education.

- *Acceptance*: This type of response focuses on taking no immediate action until the risk happens. This type of response strategy is applicable when both the negative and positive risk happen. There could be a contingency or fallback plan for this risk so that it can be accepted. External sources often make acceptance the only choice, especially when response is beyond your control. There are two main kinds of acceptance strategy: passive and active.

  - ◆ Passive acceptance indicates that no contingency plans have been created.

  - ◆ Active acceptance happens when contingency plans are developed to address that risk as it happens.

Strategies for Positive Risks or Opportunities

There are four key strategies for positive risk management:

- *Exploitation*: This response takes action to make a cause happen. Steps are taken to make sure that risk occurs, although it may require more time and resources to use this method. It is the opposite of an avoidance response.

- *Enhancing*:This type of response increases the probability of risk occurring and the impact that the risk has if it does occur. An incentive is an example of an enhanced risk response, the direct opposite of a mitigating response.

- *Sharing*: This type of response involves the help of third parties to benefit from opportunities created by positive risk events. Third party partnerships allow both sides to share the benefits, and sharing is the direct opposite of transfer response.

- *Acceptance*: Again, acceptance is a viable risk response to negative and positive risks.

Refer to the diagram at the start of the section to better orient yourself in negative and positive response strategies.

- **Contingent Response Strategies**: Sometimes events indicate that a risk is likely to happen. These are called predefined conditions, warning signs, or triggers. When a trigger happens, you must initiate or roll out your Risk Response Plan.

For example: James has prepared a Contingency Response Strategy so that he can order a batch of products from a specific vendor; let us call him vendor A. The plan sets up a shipment from vendor B if the products are more than three days late. The trigger happens when vendor A neglects to send the products within those three days. Instead of losing out on the shipment sales, they move forward thanks to the Contingency Plan.

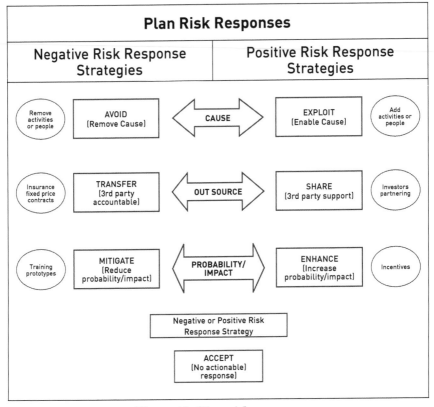

Figure 12: Plan risk responses

James has compiled the following outputs resulting from the Plan Risk Responses process:

- Project Management Plan Updates
- Project Document Updates

Learn the definition of each to fully understand the process of achieving these outputs by correctly selecting inputs and tools and techniques and then using them to inform your outcome.

Outputs to Consider with Plan Risk Responses

The Plan Risk Responses process has two outputs that you need to remember.

- *Project Management Plan Updates*: The required conclusion for Plan Risk Responses is to update the Risk Register and planned risk responses. Updating a host of additional documentation is also key to this process.
- *Project Document Updates*: Risk is part of many other areas of project management, so updating your documents is a result of Plan Risk Responses.
- *Updating the Risk Register*: At the completion of this step, you will update the Risk Owner and Risk Response sections in the Risk Register. You will also make room for Secondary Risks and Residual Risks.
- *Risk-Related Contractual Decisions*: There may be some responses that require third party support. These contractual decisions will outline this support as part of the Risk Response Plan.

Here is the Risk Register after being updated in this section:

Risk	Cause	Risk Owner	Category	Risk Response	Probability Risk Rating	Impact Risk Rating	Risk Score
		Update step 5		Update step 5	Update step 5	Update step 5	Update step 5
		Update step 5		Update step 5	Update step 5	Update step 5	Update step 5
Risk owners and responses may be updated at the conclusion of the Plan Risk Response exercise. Risk Ratings and Risk Scores may be updated based on responses developed.							

Study Success: 10 Sample Questions

Based on the information you have learned about Plan Risk Responses, answer the following questions.

1. ***What are Plan Risk Responses?***
   a. Step 5 in the process of assigning Risk Response to Risk Action Owners
   b. Step 5 in the process with the main goal of validating your risk responses
   c. Step 6 in the process, assigning planned risk to specific project goals
   d. Step 5 in the process, building a positive and negative risk list

2. ***What is the function of Risk Ownership?***
   a. To assign a risk and Plan Risk Responses for adequate Risk Management
   b. To build Contingency Plans when risks are likely to happen
   c. To enlist the assistance of Risk Action Owners as they prepare responses to risk
   d. To build a Risk Response plan with all relevant stakeholders involved

3. ***What are Residual Risks?***
   a. Risks that remain from your Risk Register after the Monitor and Control Process
   b. Risks that remain after your Risk Response Plan and Contingency Plan take effect
   c. Risks that remain from your Fallback Plan and Qualitative Risk Analysis
   d. Risks that remain from your Risk Response Plan and Decision Tree analysis

4. **Define Secondary Risk.**

   a. The risk that occurs after all original risks have been responded to

   b. Risk that starts as no-go risk and eventually becomes risk scores for your register

   c. The risk that results from a risk response and is assigned to the Risk Register

   d. The risk that happens once your level of detail has been defined on the Risk Register

5. **What factor might cause Schedule and Cost Performance Baselines to change?**

   a. Risk responses

   b. Risk owners

   c. Risk surveys/interviews

   d. Risk scores

6. **Sometimes events indicate that a risk is likely to happen soon. These are called predefined conditions or triggers. Which strategy are they part of?**

   a. Fallback Strategies

   b. Plan Risk Owner Strategies

   c. Quantitative Risk Analysis

   d. Contingency Response Strategies

7. **Name four strategies in negative risk management.**

   a. Transference, mitigation, alleviation, avoidance

   b. Acceptance, alleviation, mitigation, sharing

   c. Enhancing, transference, avoidance, acceptance

   d. Acceptance, transference, avoidance, mitigation

8. Name four key strategies in positive risk management.

a. Acceptance, mitigation, sharing, alleviation

b. Acceptance, exploitation, sharing, enhancing

c. Enhancing, mitigation, exploitation, alleviation

d. Sharing, exploitation, alleviation, acceptance

9. What is it called when you require third party support in Risk Response?

a. Contractual Decision Making

b. Risk Inclined Document Sourcing

c. Risk-Related Contractual Decisions

d. Response Related Contracts

10. What is the final output for Plan Risk Responses?

a. Project Document updates and Project Management Plan updates

b. Update Risk Register, Risk Ownership, and Qualitative Analysis

c. Update Risk Responses, Documents, and Contractual Decisions

d. Update Project Management Risk Plans

Answers:

Answer 1: B	*Answer 6:* D
Answer 2: A	*Answer 7:* D
Answer 3: B	*Answer 8:* B
Answer 4: C	*Answer 9:* C
Answer 5: A	*Answer 10:* A

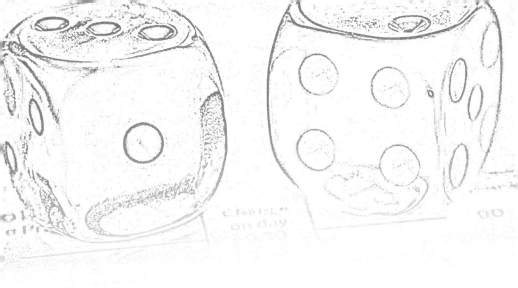

CHAPTER 11

CONTROL RISKS

"The greater danger for most of us lies
not in setting our aim too high and falling
short, but in setting our aim too low, and
achieving our mark."

MICHELANGELO

$\mathbf{P}$IER-C: With Control Risks as the final step in your Risk Management Process, the project team needs to consistently monitor and reassess risks on the Risk Register. That means implementing risk responses where you see fit. You will identify new risks, also called emergent risks, that were not identified during the Identify Risks process.

You will also need to evaluate how effective your risk program is for your overall project goals. Looking for triggers is a good practice; these are early warning signs that risk may happen. Finally, you will update your Risk Register at this stage until the project is closed.

Control Risks Explained

Defined, Control Risks is the sixth and final stage in your Risk Management Process. You have finally reached the "C" in your PIER-C process. Because risk is iterative, factors change constantly, along with conditions. Risk Management is not a one-off activity, so you need to iteratively and periodically monitor and control your risks.

Control Risks[47] is the process of maintaining risk effectiveness; tracking identified risks; identifying, analyzing, and planning for new risks; and monitoring residual and secondary risks in your Risk Register—where you will also monitor your Watch List.

In addition, at this stage, you will also reanalyze existing risks in response to change, implement Risk Response plans as they are needed, and monitor risk trigger conditions in preparation for your response implementation.

You will also submit formal changes as necessary to keep your Contingency Plans fresh while you evaluate the effectiveness of all risk responses. When you are called on to respond to a specific risk that was not identified or known, your response is called a workaround.

This process falls under the Monitoring and Controlling Process Group. The project's success frequently hinges on the project team's ability to effectively complete this process group.

The Process of Control Risks

Like the other processes, this process consists of inputs, tools and techniques, and outputs to finalize the Risk Management Plan process.

---

47   Control Risks, http://www.pm-primer.com/control-risks/

Project Risk Management in Practice!

James and his team have outlined how they plan to control risks using the following:

Inputs	Tools & Techniques	Outputs
• Project Management Plan • Risk Register • Work Performance Data • Work Performance Reports	• Risk Reassessment • Risk Audits • Variance and Trend Analysis • Technical Performance Measurement • Reserve Analysis • Meetings	• Work Performance Information • Change Requests • Project Management Plan Updates • Project Documents Updates • Organizational Process Assets Updates

If you want to be successful with the Control Risks process, you must focus on the following areas:

- *Communication*: Maintain honest and open communication with your risk owners and risk action owners to keep risks under control. Be sure to include all stakeholders when communicating risk status information, and make your project Risk Register available to a stakeholder who wants to review it. Stakeholders' input may be valuable. This proactive communication also sets expectations around risks.

- *Integration*: Make sure that the control risks process is an approved part of your Project Management Plan. Key control risks activities should be within the risk management plan; these are ongoing until the project closes.

- *Lessons Learned*: Do not forget to spend some time

recording what the project team has learned for use in future projects or by future project managers. Lessons involving both positive and negative risks need to be recorded. At each key project phase, or when you meet specific milestones, you should stop to host a lessons learned session. This facilitates progressive elaboration.

- *Awareness*: Be sure to include current risk status as an agenda item in project status meetings. The value of risk management activities needs to be promoted to help stakeholders stay informed and committed to staying actively engaged.

- *Updates*: Make sure that the Risk Register reflects all changes made, and add new risks, retire non-applicable risks, and reprioritize existing risks.

- *Reserve Management*: Do not forget to track contingency and management reserves, and make sure that you have utilized reliable metrics and formulas to calculate suitable reserves. You must request these contingency reserves as they are needed and return the reserves that are no longer required when that risk is no longer active.

Inputs to Consider With Control Risks

There are several inputs in Control Risks that you need to understand.

James has identified the following four inputs to use in Control Risks:

- Project Management Plan
- Risk Register
- Work Performance Data
- Work Performance Reports

Learn the definition of each to fully understand the inputs that drive Control Risks in project risk management.

- *Project Management Plan*: Your Project Management Plan is the approved plan that will contain your Risk Management Plan. Inside your risk management plan, you will find your roles, responsibilities, methods, and reserve considerations.
- *Risk Register*: The Risk Register gives the initial list of risks that will be evaluated. The Risk Register will be elaborated on during this stage.
- *Work Performance Data*: Work performance data may provide insight on work performance results that may have been impacted by risks.
- *Work Performance Reports*: The project's work performance reports will include Earned Value Technique data, such as cost status and schedule information. These reports will also include data used for forecasting, which is a very important part of identifying and controlling risk.

Strategies, Tools and Techniques

In the control risks process, there are a few key tools and techniques that should be used to determine predictable outcomes.

James has compiled the following six tools and techniques to perform Monitor and Control Risk with his team:

- Risk Reassessment
- Risk Audits
- Variance and Trend Analysis
- Technical Performance Measurement
- Reserve Analysis
- Meetings

Learn the definition and function of each so that you can make your own selections when you want to perform Control Risks using these tools and techniques.

- *Risk Reassessment*: Here, your Risk Reassessment pertains to the risk monitoring and control activity because it identifies new risks and existing risks that needs to be reassessed for accuracy. Many events can drive the need for risk reassessment, including project replanning, conducting phase end reviews, the occurrence of unknown risks, and changes in request evaluation. Your Risk Management plan should contain your Risk Reassessment requirements.

- *Risk Audits*: A risk audit actively looks at your responses to risk and determines how well you did with that risk. They measure the overall impact of your Risk Management Process. That is why risk audits should be conducted periodically—so that you can evaluate weaknesses and strengths in your overall Risk Management Process. These risk audit requirements are identified in your Risk Management Plan.

- *Variance and Trend Analysis*: Deviations and trends need to be noted, and your planned results must be compared with your actual ones.

- *Technical Performance Measurement*: Your quality management plan defines your metrics and targets, among other things. It determines if your actual technical performance achieved matches with the technical performance specifications that you have planned.

- *Reserve Analysis*: Contingency reserves and management reserves for risks are typically granted in complex projects. If they are, the project manager will usually manage the contingency reserves and make sure that they are only allocated if a risk event happens. Management reserves are usually not under the direct control of the project manager. Unknown risks, also called *unknown unknowns*, are designated in management reserves. Known risks, also called *known unknowns*, are designated for your contingency reserves.

- *Meetings*: Some of your status meetings or an entirely separate meeting are needed to address risk. All risk should be considered to be important rather than as a side element. PMI actively recommends that you and your team host a meeting once a week about risk. These periodic meetings will let your stakeholders identify new risks throughout your project and risk management process.

Outputs to Consider With Control Risks

The Control Risks process must include change requests and updates as key outputs of this process.

James has compiled the following outputs resulting from the Control Risks process:

- Work Performance Information
- Change Requests
- Project Management Plan Updates
- Project Documents Updates
- Organizational Process Asset Updates

Learn the definition of each to fully understand the process of achieving these outputs by correctly selecting inputs and tools and techniques and using them to inform your outcome.

- **_Work Performance Information_:** This information becomes a valuable source for both communicating as well as supporting project decisions.

Defined, a change request[8] is a document that calls for an adjustment in the system that is of importance. It clearly states what needs to be accomplished. This excludes how the change will be conducted.

- **_Change Requests_:** Preventative or corrective change requests may be needed so that contingency plans and fallback plans can be formally changed through perform integrated change control. If the project needs to comply with the Project Management Plan, a change request may also be filed. This helps mitigate Gold Plating and Scope Creep, both of which are discussed in Chapter 13.

- *Project Management Plan and Document Updates*: Living documents, that is, documents that are constantly changing and evolving, like the Risk Management Plan and Risk Register, may also need to be updated at this stage.

- *Organizational Process Asset Updates*: If lessons learned have prompted fresh insight, risk breakdown structures need to be updated. There could be many other project management templates that also need to be updated as part of your organizational process asset updates.

Taking all of these elements into account will allow the project team to work through the process of Control Risks as well as enable you to monitor already identified risks, identify new risks, ensure proper plan execution, and evaluate the overall efficiency of the risk management plan—thereby reducing overall project risk.

Study Success: 10 Sample Questions

Based on the information you have learned about Control Risks, answer the following questions.

1. What four main features does Control Risks encompass?

    a. Plan for new risks, monitor residual and secondary risks, track identified risks, maintain effectiveness of risk responses

    b. Monitor residual and secondary risks, update contingency plans, formalize planning process groups, update the Risk Register

    c. Track identified risks, monitor new risks, control change plans, improve the risk management process

    d. Stakeholder involvement, risk monitoring, efficiency tracking, Risk Register updates

2. Which of these is a component of Control Risks?

    a. Submitting organizational process documents for review

    b. Submitting formal changes to keep your contingency plan relevant

    c. Conducting an in-depth audit of your stakeholder schedules

    d. Performing a Quantitative Risk Analysis several times

3. Which statement is true?

    a. Honest and open communication is critical for risk owners.

    b. Monitor and control processes need to be approved.

c. Your risk management plan contains your key activities in this section.

d. All of the above

4. *How do you prevent negative history from recurring and cause positive history to recur more often?*

a. By filing a change plan

b. By performing consistent updates on your documents

c. By hosting periodic lessons learned meetings

d. By focusing on individual project phases as they happen

5. *Name the four inputs in Control Risks.*

a. Project management plan, organizational process assets, risk register, change reports

b. Work performance information, risk register, risk tracking, organizational process assets

c. Work performance reports, work performance data, risk register, project management plan

d. Organizational process assets, work performance information, risk reviews, risk reassessment

6. *Identify four of the six tools and techniques in Control Risks.*

a. Risk audits, meetings, reserve analysis, risk reassessment

b. Risk analysis, risk trends, risk reassessment, status meetings

   c. Risk reassessment, risk audits, status meetings, risk documents

   d. Risk trends, risk documents, risk audits, reserve analysis

7. **Define Risk Reassessment.**

   a. It identifies risks that need reassessment for inclusion in a decision tree.

   b. It identifies variances and trends and then uses them to re-determine risk.

   c. It identifies your responses to that risk then reassesses them over time.

   d. It identifies new risks and existing risks that need to be reassessed for accuracy.

8. **Match unknown unknowns and known unknowns to the correct reserve analysis.**

   a. Unknown unknowns, management reserves. Known unknowns, contingency reserves.

   b. Known unknowns, reserve analysis. Unknown unknowns, management reserves.

   c. Unknown unknowns, contingency reserves. Known unknowns, management reserves.

   d. Unknown unknowns, management reserves. Known unknowns, contingency plans.

9. **What needs to be updated in your organizational process documents?**

   a. Risk breakdown structures

   b. Risk Register

    c. Risk audits

    d. Work performance information

10. *What are change requests used for?*

    a. To correct work performance data to maintain accuracy

    b. To prevent or correct contingency or fallback plans

    c. To update the Risk Register for the next phase

    d. To control risks as part of your organizational plan

Answers:

Answer 1: A

Answer 2: B

Answer 3: D

Answer 4: C

Answer 5: C

Answer 6: A

Answer 7: D

Answer 8: A

Answer 9: A

Answer 10: B

CHAPTER 12

RISK GOVERNANCE

"Perhaps when a man has special
knowledge and special powers like my own,
it rather encourages him to seek a complex
explanation when a simpler one is at hand."

**ARTHUR CONAN DOYLE
(SHERLOCK HOLMES)**

Within the PMI-RMP® Body of Knowledge, there is a Risk Governance area. Once you have conducted project risk analysis and performed your PIER-C, you will need to understand how to govern these processes during the project.

That is why Risk Governance follows Control Risks, even though it is outside the PIER-C process, as a standalone practice. This chapter will help you understand what it is and how it should be used to support your risk management strategy.

What Is Risk Governance?

Defined, Risk Governance is the process of making sure that your risk procedures and policies are understood, adhered to, consistently applied, and highly effective. That is why Risk Governance is implemented by the project manager, another project manager on your team, or a specialized organizational Risk Governance body. Ownership of Risk Governance is based on the project's importance, size, and priority for the company.

Once you have completed your PIER-C analysis, you will need to focus on Risk Governance. It is useful to learn some key concepts in this area so that you fully understand how it works.

In Risk Governance, you will use the tools, techniques, and outputs from the Control Risks process. To recap, review this brief summary.

Tools and techniques commonly used in risk governance:

- Risk Reassessment
- Risk Audits
- Variance and Trend Analysis
- Technical Performance Measurement
- Reserve Analysis
- Meetings

Outputs commonly created after risk governance:

- Work Performance Information
- Organizational Process Asset Updates
- Change Requests
- Project Management Plan and Document Updates

These come from the Control Risks process.

Why Does Risk Governance Matter?

Risk governance takes a careful look at the complicated network of policies, procedures, rules, actors, and methods that are used in risk information gathering, analysis, and communication—and how decisions are made.

Effective project risk governance is all about consistent risk assessment, management, and communication. These three elements ensure that project risks are kept under control, are monitored regularly, and are updated as needed to produce current plans that work.

That is why risk governance ensures that the project goals and the objectives of the Board of Directors and other key stakeholders are in alignment. It may include the creation of standard practices and procedures so that risk compliance is all but guaranteed.

Standard policies and procedures may impact:

- The required levels of sponsorship that are based on key considerations, such as portfolio level priorities and projects.
- Areas like risk processes, organizational process assets, resource breakdown structures, and standard templates.
- Risk category thresholds and organizational risk tolerance standards in addition to standardized quality management planning that includes targets and metrics and a Process Improvement Plan.
- The creation of metrics to help guide organizational management activities across all levels of analysis.
- The standardized risk management planning, including risk breakdown structures and risk identification methods. Governance may also cause the standard processing of lessons learned at each stage of the Risk Management Process. Data gathering and standard corporate knowledge base direction should also be influenced by the Risk Governance policy.
- The standardized policies and procedures relating to Risk Reassessment, Risk Audits, and Risk Reviews will similarly be impacted.
- Finally, policies and procedures, which will assist in conducting and sharing lessons learned; this will involve what went well and where you can do better in the next project cycle along with what can be done differently for a potential improvement in project results.

Your Role in Risk Governance

The project risk manager plays an essential role in risk governance. You need to be aware that there are two main organizations that impact Risk Governance in general.

- The first is the International Risk Governance Council (IRGC). Your risk governance may have to follow its principles. This organization has a primary goal—to facilitate your understanding of and help you manage risks that impact society, safety, human health, and the environment overall.

- The second organization is called the International Organization for Standardization (ISO). PMI is aligned with ISO standards, which are based on best practices from across the globe. In order to meet organizational needs, Risk Governance ensures that risk management efforts are focused and standardized. It makes sure that your organization and project team have a cultural norm that supports project risk management activities.

- All projects require a Risk Governance structure. This helps project managers successfully control and manage their project, a structure that ensures that all internal controls are adhered to and involves a complex set of relationships between you as the project manager and your team and key stakeholders.

- Project risks are continually evolving, and without a formal governance system in place, there will be conflict and confusion related to changes associated with risks. As project complexity increases, so will your need for a more stringent governance model.

Risk Governance Concepts to Understand

Earned Value Technique is the recommended primary method of performance reporting. In Risk Governance, performance reporting is a key concern. In order to successfully understand and calculate using the Earned Value Technique, a few key terms need to be defined.

- EV (Earned Value) is the measure of work performed expressed in terms of the budget authorized for that work.

> 65% of a $100,000 project is finished.
> Multiply .65 × $100,000 to determine the EV.
>
> .65 × $100,000 = $65,000
> EV = $65,000

- PV (Planned Value) is the authorized budget assigned to scheduled work at a specific time. For example, let us say the project at this point should be 70% complete.

> 70% complete in a $100,000 project.
> Multiply .7 × $100,000 to determine the PV.
>
> .7 × $100,000 = $70,000
> PV = $70,000

- AC (Actual Cost) is the realized cost incurred for the work performed on an activity during a specific time period. The actual cost for the example above is $75,000, which is the amount actually spent to date.
- BAC (Budget at Completion) is a term used to describe the total budget for your project. For this specific scenario, imagine that your BAC is $100,000.

- SV (Schedule Variance) with a value of 0 is representative of a project that is on schedule. A negative SV indicates that the project is behind schedule. You will see in the example below that the -$5000 indicates that the project is behind schedule. A positive SV indicates that it is ahead of schedule.

- CV (Cost Variance) with a value of 0 is representative of the project being on budget. A negative CV indicates that the project is behind budget. The example below of -$10,000 indicates that the project is behind budget. A positive CV indicates that the project is ahead of budget.

- SPI (Schedule Performance Index) of 1.0 indicates that the project is on schedule. An SPI with an index of less than 1.0 indicates that the project is behind schedule. The example below of .93 proves that the project is behind schedule. An SPI of more than 1.0 indicates that the project is ahead of schedule.

- CPI (Cost Performance Index) of 1.0 indicates that the project is on budget. A CPI of less than 1.0 indicates that the project is behind budget. The example below of .87 means that the project is behind budget. A CPI of more than 1.0 indicates that the project is ahead of budget.

- ETC (Estimate to Completion): In the below scenario, the project is behind on both the schedule and the budget. The ETC based on the current trend is therefore $114,943. This means that there is a cost overrun of $14,943—unless the project manager takes action to counter this worsening situation.

Here is the project example:

A rundown of the results so far in this example would be:
- EV = $65,000
- PV = $70,000
- AC = $75,000
- BAC = $100,000

These values are then used to calculate variance.

Earned Value Technique Calculation	Formula
SV: Schedule Variance	Earned Value (EV) – Planned Value (PV) $65,000 – $70,000 = -$5000
CV: Cost Variance	Earned Value (EV) – Actual Costs (AC) $65,000 – $75,000 = -$10,000
SPI: Schedule Performance Index	Earned Value (EV) / Planned Value (PV) $65,000 / $70,000 = .93
CPI: Cost Performance Index	Earned Value (EV) / Actual Value (AV) $65,000 / $75,000 = .87
ETC: Estimate to Completion	Budget at Completion (BAC) / Cost Performance Index (CPI) $100,000 / .87 = $114,943

Governance Areas of Note

As part of their Risk Governance policies and procedures, some organizations dictate specific contract type requirements. For the test, you should know who assumes the Cost Risk for the contracts that are detailed below.

- *Cost Reimbursable*: The total costs are not known until the very end of that contract; therefore, the Cost Risk is on the buyer. A Cost Reimbursable Contract involves payments to the seller for all legitimate actual costs incurred for completed work. Cost Plus Percentage of Cost (CPPC) poses the greatest Cost Risk to the buyer.
- *Fixed Price*: A Fixed Price Contract is a type of contract where the buyer pays the seller a set amount as defined by the contract. The Cost Risk is primarily on the seller. A Fixed Price Contract is typically used when a project service or product is clearly defined. The seller will provide a price proposal to perform work as described by the potential buyer. The Fixed Price Contract can be adjusted over time. A Firm Fixed Price, or FFP, Contract is a much stricter version of the basic Fixed Price Contract. The FFP Contract is almost never changed or altered. In this case, the contract price may remain unchanged for the entire life of the contract.
- *Time and Material*: A contract type that is a hybrid contractual arrangement containing aspects of both cost-reimbursable and fixed-price contracts.

Study Success: 10 Sample Questions

Based on the information you have learned about Risk Governance, answer the following questions.

1. *Where does Risk Governance come into the PIER-C Process?*

   b. It comes in before Monitoring and Control.

   c. It is a standalone process, outside of PIER-C.

   d. It comes in after Quantitative Risk Analysis.

   e. It comes in before Plan Risk Response.

2. *Define Risk Governance.*

   a. The process of ensuring that your risk procedure policies are understood and effective

   b. The process of ensuring that your Risk Governance body is adhered to

   c. The process of governing all of your risks within PIER-C

   d. The process of using inputs, tools and techniques, and outputs to manage risk

3. *Name three tools and techniques used in Risk Governance.*

   a. Change Requests, Reserve Analysis, Risk Audits

   b. Risk Review, Change Requests, Risk Reassessment

   c. Reserve Analysis, Technical Performance Measurement, Risk Audits

   d. Risk Register, Status Meetings, Rusk Audits

4. Why does Risk Governance matter?

   a. It looks at a network of methods, policies, actors, and procedures to see how decisions are being made.

   b. It ensures that your Board of directors see that your goals and objectives are met.

   c. It serves to govern content risk assessment, management, and communication.

   d. All of the above

5. Which areas will Risk Governance impact?

   a. Risk processes, organizational process asset, and standard templates

   b. Quantitative and qualitative analysis calculations

   c. The role of your Risk Team in schedule management and estimations

   d. All of the above

6. Which two organizations affect Risk Governance?

   a. International Standards Organization and The Risk Management Council

   b. International Risk Governance Council and International Organization for Standardization

   c. International Risk Governance Council and International Organization for Systems Change

   d. International Risk Organization and International Standards Organization

7. **What is Earned Value?**
   a. The value of work performed
   b. The cost of work estimated
   c. The value of pending costs
   d. The value of work to be determined

8. **What does AC stand for?**
   a. Actuary Costs
   b. Accented Costs
   c. Actual Costs
   d. Accurate Costs

9. **What does it mean if a project has a negative CV?**
   a. The project is behind budget.
   b. The project is ahead of schedule.
   c. The project is behind schedule.
   d. The project is ahead of budget.

10. **Calculate Schedule Variance: EV = $50,000; PV = $60,000.**
   a. $10,000
   b. .83
   c. .10
   d. -$10,000

Answers:

Answer 1: B	*Answer 6:* B
Answer 2: A	*Answer 7:* A
Answer 3: C	*Answer 8:* C
Answer 4: D	*Answer 9:* A
Answer 5: A	*Answer 10:* D

CHAPTER 13

RISK MANAGEMENT IMPORTANT CONCEPTS

"It seems that the necessary thing to do is not to fear mistakes, to plunge in, to do the best that one can, hoping to learn enough from blunders to correct them eventually."

ABRAHAM MASLOW

The PMBOK Guide encompasses a large volume of knowledge, and there are many concepts discussed within its pages. For those looking to gain their PMI-RMP® qualification, it is critical to have a firm grasp on the concepts of project management as outlined in The PMBOK Guide.

Important Concepts for Project Management

The four most important areas at the beginning of The PMBOK Guide are outlined here.

- PMI Process Groups
- Integrated Change Control Functions
- The Types of Organizations
- Understanding Project Environments

PMI Process Groups

Within the PMI Framework, you need to know the five Process Groups in order, starting with Initiating and ending with Closing. Here they are in graphical form:

Figure 13: Process groups within PMI framework

Integrated Change Control

Integrated change control is an important concept to remember, so keep these guidelines in mind for the test.

- Create a change control log. This lists all of change requests that are processed in support of your project. The status of your changes is also provided in this log, including those that have been both denied and approved. Review your Change Control Log because it may be a source of risks.
- An Integrated Change Control procedure should be defined for each project. That means your procedures for reviewing these changes must identify new risks that could be introduced via a recommended change.
- The Perform Integrated Change Control process should communicate approval or denial of these recommended changes.
- Perform Integrated Change Control is also part of Configuration Management. It focuses on controlling changes to your physical and functional project's product, service, or result characteristics.

Types of Organizations

There are three main organizational structures:

- *Functional:* The most common Functional form is characterized by staff members being grouped by specialty, with each employee having one manager, siloed organizational functions, and team members that communicate between these siloes.
- *Matrix:* This form is characterized by a blend of functional and projectized organizations where some or all resources are borrowed from functional units. Team members report to two supervisors: the functional manager and the project manager. The core matrix types are strong,

balanced, and weak. The default for PMI questions is a strong matrix organization.

- *Projectized:* The third form is typically characterized by colocated (resources in a single location) team members. Personnel that are assigned report to a project manager, where the organizational focus is on projects and project managers have high levels of independence and authority. Colocation is also known as tight matrix.

Understanding Project Environments

- *International and Political Environments:* Understand current political climates, and familiarize yourself with applicable laws.
- *Physical Environment:* The physical environment in which you work matters, so learn to consider how it will be impacted during your project.
- *Cultural and Social Environments:* Learn to recognize how your project impacts people and how people impact your project. Not addressing these environments can lead to a lack of stakeholder buy-in with overall project goals.

Important Concepts for Project Scope Management

Project Scope Management is discussed in chapter 5 of *The PMBOK Guide*.

The most critical concepts are detailed below:

- Scope Baseline
- Scope Statement
- Scope Creep and Gold Plating
- Work Breakdown Structure (WBS)
- Work Breakdown Structure Dictionary

- *Scope Baseline:* This is an important input that supports many risk management activities. Scope baseline is comprised of three basic components: scope statement, work breakdown structure (WBS), and WBS dictionary.
- *Scope Statement:* Your scope statement is a defined version of your project deliverables, which means that it helps to define the type of project you are running. It can be a recurring project, which will make risk easier to manage, or it may introduce new variables, thus increasing the level of risk management complexity.
- *Scope Creep*: This term refers to the changes in your project scope that are not processed through the formal integrated change control process. Gold plating on projects usually refers to the process or concept of the project team itself adding functionality beyond what is covered by the requirements. Both scope creep and gold plating are to be avoided.
- *Work Breakdown Structure (WBS)*: A work breakdown structure is a hierarchical decomposition of the project's work packages and activities that must be completed. You will need to update it to reflect additional work required for your risk responses. It is a tool in risk management that allows you to identify and track risks at the work package, control account, and summary levels.
- A Work Breakdown Structure Dictionary defines the activities and work packages in the WBS.

Important Concepts for Project Time Management

Chapter 6 in *The PMBOK Guide* covers project time management.

The most important concepts are detailed below:
- Key Documents Produced from Project Time Management
- Estimating Methods
- Sources of Conflict
- Buffer Analysis

Key Documents Produced From Project Time Management

These are the documents that are created and completed during Project Time Management that actively influence the Risk Management Process.

- *Schedule Baseline*: This is the primary output for project time management and represents project schedules that have been approved. It can be adjusted through the formal Integrated Change Control process, which accounts for risk.

- *Project Schedule Network Diagrams*: These are created during sequence activities and show key dependencies while providing a visual view of potential path convergence problems. These diagrams are also an input for Monte Carlo analysis.

- *Resource Breakdown Structure*: This is an output of estimate activity resources. It shows which resources are needed for the project, which makes it an important document that is used during Identify Risks.

Estimating Methods

Estimating methods are broken down into three main types—analogous, parametric, and bottom up—and understanding their characteristics is essential.

- *Bottom up*: Analyzes data at work package and activity level with the information provided by those conducting the work. This requires effort, time, and a comprehensive WBS. One of the risks associated with a bottom up estimate is padding by the team members.
- *Parametric*: This is an objective estimating method that uses numerical data for estimations. It must be used with accurate and reliable numerical data for best results. One concern with parametric estimates is that historical project records do not always reflect current market conditions.
- *Analogous*: This is also called top down estimating. It is a big picture in which the actual cost of a previous project is taken as the basis for estimating cost for the current project. Experts can relatively quickly provide an approximate estimate with a limited amount of detailed information about the project. A risk is that the projects may not be comparable.

Sources of Conflict

In project time management, the main source of conflict encountered is due to scheduling issues.

Buffer Analysis

Defined, a buffer is a non-working time that is added between two exercises or activities to account for risks that have been identified. For example, launch a product, wait four days for the metrics, and then begin on-site testing. The buffer here is the four-day wait. These are used along with Critical Chain Methods when the project manager is aware of constraints before the final project schedule is solidified.

Important Concepts for Project Quality Management

Chapter 8 of *The PMBOK Guide* covers Project Quality Management. A project's quality standards impact Risk Governance and Analysis. The Quality Management Plan is an important input for the Identify Risks process.

From these inputs come a range of outputs in your Quality Management Plan that are defined below:

- Quality Management Plan
- Quality Metrics
- Quality Checklists
- Project Document Updates
- Process Improvement Plan

- *Quality Standards*: Ask what quality standards apply to the project and how your project team will ensure they are met. For example: OSHA: Safety, ISO 9000 recommended quality standards, industry standards and codes, and Sarbanes-Oxley.

- *Quality Metrics*: Ask what metrics should be measured and if these metrics are SMART, as in *specific, measurable, accountable, realistic,* and *time-sensitive.*

- *Quality Checklists*: Ask what steps you should take to perform specific verifications and which quality checklists will support your project end goals.

- *Quality Assurance*: Asks which standards will be assessed to prevent future issues and how changes and any preventative actions will be dealt with

- *Quality Control*: Asks how inspections will be managed, how they will be measured and reported on, and how changes and corrective actions will be dealt with

- *Responsibilities*: Asks who will help you manage your project quality control and what their specific quality-based responsibilities will be
- *Targets*: Ask what your current performance levels are that need improvement during your project.
- *Process Improvement Plan*: Asks how you will identify wasteful and non-valuable activities so that they can be reported on

Review these key concepts about project quality management to understand the activity involved in this vital process.

Important Concepts for Project Human Resource Management

Chapter 9 of *The PMBOK Guide* covers Project Human Resource Management.

Here are some important concepts:

- Motivational Theory
- Maslow's Hierarchy of Needs Theory
- Expectancy Theory
- Achievement Motivation Theory
- McGregor's Theory X and Y
- Hertzberg's Theory
- Leadership Styles
- Directive
- Facilitative
- Consensus Building
- Autocratic

- Consultative
- Coaching
- Supporting
- Tuckman Model
- Forming
- Storming
- Norming
- Performing
- Adjourning
- Leadership Style Applicability
- Situation and Style Table
- Negotiation Methods
- Functional Manager
- Stakeholder Negotiation

Understand these concepts for a stronger grasp of Project Human Resource Management.

Motivational Theory

- *Maslow's Hierarchy of Needs Theory*: This theory states that motivation happens in a hierarchical manner. Simply put, each level must be attained before moving on to the next. The levels are physiological, safety, social, esteem, and self-actualization.
- *Expectancy Theory*: This is when your employees believe that effort leads to performance. This performance needs to be rewarded based on individual expectations because rewards improve productivity.
- *Achievement Motivation Theory*: This theory by David McClelland states that three needs must be met for

people to be satisfied: achievement, affiliation, and power.

- *Herzberg's Theory:* This theory states that there are hygiene factors and motivating agents. Hygiene factors include working conditions, benefits, and salary; shortfalls in these areas are believed to destroy motivation. Motivating factors like achievement, growth, and responsibility increase motivation.

- *McGregor's Theory X and Y:* This theory defines how all employees fit into one of two groups. Theory X managers believe that people cannot be trusted and should be watched at all times. Theory Y managers believe that people can be trusted because they want to achieve success and they are self-motivated.

Leadership Styles

These leadership styles affect stakeholder support of the Risk Management Process, so they must be used according to a project's unique circumstances.

- *Directive:* As the leader, you tell others what to do.
- *Facilitative:* As the leader, you coordinate and solicit input from other people.
- *Consensus Building:* As the leader, you solve problems based on team input and seek decision buy-in and agreement.
- *Autocratic:* As the leader, you make decisions without input from other people.
- *Consultative:* As the leader, you invite others to input their ideas.
- *Coaching:* As the leader, you train others in how to perform the work at hand.
- *Supporting:* As the leader, you provide assistance and support as needed to your team to achieve the project goals.

Tuckman Model

The Tuckman model is an often used five-step model utilized to show the growth of your team from the moment it is created. Teams work through these step-by-step growth processes, so you can use a model like this to determine the suitable leadership style to employ at a given point in time.

- *Forming*: A new team meets and learns about your project. Productivity is low as roles are determined, and you can expect hesitation, confusion, anxiety, and lack of direction at this stage.
- *Storming*: Your team starts to work together, addressing project management approaches and technical issues and work. Productivity may decrease due to disruptive conflict if cliques form and your leadership is challenged.
- *Norming*: Your team members are working together, accommodating their team by adjusting their habits and adhering to open lines of communication, purpose, motivation, and confidence. Productivity at this stage does improve.
- *Performing*: Your team members are independent and self-directed. They work through things quickly and easily because of their existing trust and pride. Productivity peaks at this stage.
- *Adjourning*: All work is completed as the project winds down and the team moves on.

Leadership Style Applicability

All leadership styles can be used to support any number of project management situations. Learn the recommendations for the scenarios below.

- Situation and Style Table:

Appropriate Leadership Style	Scenario / Situation
Coaching, Directive	Your team is new and just forming; they need task orientation and direction from you.
Consultative, Facilitative, Consensus Building	Your team is storming, and there is a great deal of conflict, frustration, and confusion.
Autocratic	Your team needs decisions to be made quickly because time is pivotal. There is little time for input from others.
Supporting	Your team is well-established and skilled; they are performing work stages with ease.

Negotiation Methods

One of the key interpersonal skills as a project manager is negotiation, and you need to use it, along with influencing, to get positive results.

- *Functional Manager:* This term is applied to managers that own the human resources in a functional area. The project manager will negotiate with the functional manager to get support and resources. These managers may not always be willing to help, as they may be associated competing projects in an organization.

Stakeholder Negotiation

Your ability to influence multiple stakeholders to obtain the necessary support for the project risk management plan is critical.

- Whenever possible, take a collaborative approach.
- Be willing to compromise and remain flexible if circumstances allow it.
- Focus on relationship building to find out how to assist your stakeholders, and build in win–win situations in return for their support.
- Recognize that your stakeholders have other work to do, so be realistic about demands and help where you can.
- Know that you need to be able to explain your project in detail and in simple terms. Work on the who, what, when, where, and why impacts that affect risks.
- Explain business needs to gain support; your functional manager may not see the project risks or benefits, so enlighten them.

Important Concepts for Project Communications Management

Chapter 10 of *The PMBOK Guide* covers the Project Communications Management concepts.

Here are important concepts defined below:
- The Communications Management Plan
- Calculating Communication Channels
- The Communications Model
- Lessons Learned

The Communications Management Plan

This plan is an important document that helps support your Risk Management Process. It needs to define who needs to receive risk related communications—like responses, status, meetings, and so forth.

- *Who:* Ask with whom you should communicate, who owns the communication item, who addresses stakeholder communications, who receives information and is responsible for the confirmation of that information, and who authorizes communication.
- *What:* Ask what information needs to be communicated.
- *When and Where:* Ask when your communication should happen, what the ideal frequency of that communication might be, and where the communication will happen.
- *How:* Ask which media, language, methods, and technology will be used in communication. Ask about formats, templates, and version control. Ask whether you need flowcharts for clarity.
- *Why:* Ask why your communication is important and why your receiver should care. Outline the value proposition for your communication.

Calculating Communication Channels

There is a formula for calculating the number of your communication channels. You need to remember this formula for the test.

Communications Channels = n(n−1)/2

Example: With a value of 8 stakeholders

8(8−1)/2 = 28 channels

You can see that 28 channels of communication exist, which means there may be 28 different interpretations of a key project item. Your goal is to remove rumors and maintain the reality of the project.

The Communications Model

Take some time to understand this communications model for your test.

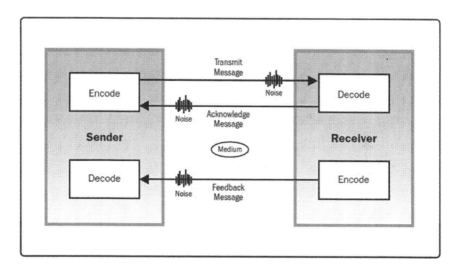

Figure 14: A Communications Model[48]

- Sender must encode the message and choose the correct medium to get it to the receiver (email, fax, etc.)

---

48   PMP Series: Project Communication Management, http://resources. intenseschool.com/pmp-series-project-communication-management/

- Receiver must decode the message and choose the correct medium for feedback.
- Feedback is the core output of encoding.
- Noise can distort transmission and/or understanding or block messages—these are called communication blockers.
- Communications management seeks to overcome these noise factors, which can cause conflict.

Lessons Learned

The core goal of lessons learned is to assist in the future project manager's performance. Sometimes called *Post Mortem*, these are accomplished at the end of the project phase and support the risk management process.

- Past risk communication lessons learned provides you with ideas on how you can improve the next project.
- Lessons learned also improve risk analysis and save future project teams hours of research and assumption risk.
- Always review past risk responses and Contingency Plans—focus on what was done properly and what can be done better, and improve everything.
- Lessons learned should be conducted after your project as a priority so that it is still fresh in the minds of your team.
- Refine policies and practices as you uncover lessons learned and incorporate best practices into future Risk Governance plans.

Important Concepts for Project Stakeholder Management

Chapter 13 of *The PMBOK Guide* covers the Project Stakeholder Management concepts.

> The important concept in this chapter related to risk management is the process to identify stakeholders.
>
> • Identify Stakeholders

Identify Stakeholders

A great project manager spends 90% of their time on communication. Communication skills are the most important interpersonal skill that will impact your project success.

Identify Stakeholders uses this two-step approach:

Step 1: Identifies stakeholders and finalizes a stakeholder register, which is developed via brainstorming and interviews. The stakeholder register is used to identify stakeholders that should be involved in risk management activities.

> A stakeholder register includes identification of all stakeholders, their needs, requirements, expectations, roles, and responsibilities.

Step 2: The second step is to develop a Stakeholder Management Strategy. Review the methods to accomplish this output using the very common power/interest model, which suggests that shareholders with varying degrees of power and interest should be dealt with differently. For example, monitoring shareholders with little interest or power requires the least amount of effort; those with low power and high interest should be kept informed, and, finally, the high power/high interest stakeholders should be closely monitored and receive frequent updates.[49] You can also use the Salience model, which focuses on power, urgency, and legitimacy of your stakeholder actions.

Having a firm grasp on this information will help you pass the test the first time. Review the past chapters, and then take the sample question challenge!

---

49   Stakeholder Power/Interest Analysis, http://requirementstechniques. wordpress.com/stakeholder-analysis/stakeholder-powerinterest-analysis/

CHAPTER 14
THE SAMPLE QUESTION CHALLENGE

Well done! You have worked your way through the study guide and have arrived at the test segment. This section will thoroughly test your knowledge on what you have just learned. With focus, you will pass your PMI-RMP® Exam on the first try!

1.	What is project management?	
a.	The process of reducing risk by planning a project based on a set of principles.	
b.	The ability to manage projects within specific parameters using Quantitative and Qualitative Analysis tools.	
c.	The process of planning and organizing an organization's resources in order to move a specific task, event, or duty toward completion.	
d.	The process of preparing a strategy to improve an organization's budget.	

2.	How many processes does project risk management entail?	
a.	7	
b.	8	
c.	5	
d.	6	

3.	Define Project Risk Management.	
a.	It involves practices that focus on aligning risks with business goals.	
b.	It involves processes that identify, analyze, and respond to many risk factors.	
c.	It involves processes that track, analyze, and record risks as they happen.	
d.	It involves creating successful projects based on forecasting risk.	

4.	What is your most important role as a project risk manager?	
a.	To prepare for risks that may arise during your project	
b.	To create calculations and formulas that determine where risk lies	
c.	To make sure that your Risk Team is focused on uncovering risks	
d.	To identify risk and determine how it will impact or impede your project	

5.	Which three concerns help define your role as a project manager?	
a.	Planning risk responses, managing your team, estimating values	
b.	Building risk management plans, establishing governance, building infrastructure	
c.	Monitoring and controlling risk, identifying risk, calculating variances	

d.	Building risk management plans, Performing qualitative risk analysis, Performing quantitative risk analysis	

6.	**Define the risk management process.**	
a.	The process of comprehending the nature of risk to determine the level of risk posed	
b.	The systematic application of management procedures and practices involved in the activity of communicating, establishing the context for, and identifying, analyzing, evaluating, treating, monitoring, and reviewing risk	
c.	A tool for ranking and displaying risks by defining ranges for consequence and likelihood	
d.	Defining internal and external parameters to be taken into account when mitigating risk and setting scope and criteria for the risk management policy	

7.	**What is a Risk Management Plan?**	
a.	Understanding risk and planning to identify, analyze, monitor, and control that risk is all part of your role as a project risk manager. To do this effectively, you need to know how to build a functional plan.	
b.	The document that you will prepare, which will enable you to foresee risks, estimate impacts from this risk, and define responses to it that address the core problems in that risk. Within this document is a risk assessment matrix.	

c.	The method of governing and guiding the eventual execution of all of your Project Risk Management processes	
d.	The level of risk without taking existing systems and procedures into account to control or manage risk	

8.	What does PIER-C stand for?	
a.	Plan, Identify, Estimate, Recall, Control	
b.	Process, Identify, Evaluate, Respond, Calculation	
c.	Plan, Identify, Estimate, Respond, Control	
d.	Plan, Identify, Evaluate, Respond, Control	

9.	Name the three-step approach to analysis in project risk management.	
a.	Inputs, tools and techniques, outputs	
b.	Positive, negative, most likely	
c.	Biased, unbiased, conservative	
d.	Identify, analyze, respond	

10.	Name three Plan Risk Management inputs.	
a.	Organizational process assets, qualitative analysis, enterprise environmental factors, project scope statement	
b.	Enterprise environmental factors, risk maintenance plan, organizational process assets, cost management plan	

c.	Organizational process assets, Risk Register, schedule management plan, cost management plan	
d.	Project scope statement, communications management plan, cost management plan, schedule management plan	

11. Who should be involved in Plan Risk Management meetings?

a.	The project risk manager	
b.	Key stakeholders and stakeholders with risk responsibility	
c.	Subject matter expert and team members	
d.	All of the above	

12. What is a Risk Threshold?

a.	A measure of what your stakeholder is willing to accept. They are shown as figures or percentages and help determine responses to that risk.	
b.	Describes an individual or organizations willingness to accept risk	
c.	Ensure that all policies and procedures are followed and tend to key governance criteria and methods	
d.	Categorize risk to group them based on common causes. This makes risk response easier.	

13.	What is a Risk Register?	
a.	A document that sources perspectives from stakeholders and multiple sources to get their commitment	
b.	A risk management tool that is commonly used in project management and organizational risk assessments. It is a central place where all risks can be identified by the project team.	
c.	The method that enables you to identify and describe risk. Use a three-step method to develop a risk statement: cause, risk, and effect.	
d.	A tool that makes sure all policies and procedures are followed and tends to key governance criteria and methods	

14.	A scope baseline is an input involved in Identify Risk. What does it include?	
a.	The scope baseline includes your activity cost estimates, WBS, and the cost management plan.	
b.	The scope baseline includes your scope statement, WBS and the dictionary you will use with your WBS.	
c.	The scope baseline includes your scope statement, stakeholder register, and the dictionary you will use with your risk management plan.	
d.	The scope baseline includes your risk statement, WBS, and activity cost and duration estimates.	

15.	What is a stakeholder register?	
a.	A register that contains important information on your stakeholders, like their identification information, classification, and assessment information	
b.	A register that contains project documents, controls, lessons learned, historical information, and your templates	
c.	A register that contains metrics, standards, checklists for quality control, targets, and process improvement opportunities that you identify	
d.	A register that contains studies, checklists, published information, industry studies, benchmarking, and risk attitudes that are pertinent to the project	

16.	Define documentation review.	
a.	It is made up of the lessons learned that allow you to create lists that support a number of different projects.	
b.	A register that contains important information on your stakeholders, like their identification information, classification, and assessment information	
c.	It requires that you read through all of your project documentation to make sure that it is easily understood and clear.	

d.	Project documents include your assumption log, earned value technique metrics, work performance reports, baselines, and any network diagrams that are relevant.	

17.	**What is an influence diagram?**	
a.	A diagram that shows the potential risk factor for that cause and the effect that it may bring about. These are also called Fishbone Diagrams or Ishikawa Diagrams.	
b.	Similar to brainstorming, input is collected from a specific group, which is then analyzed and rank ordered by the group.	
c.	A process flowchart that shows how systems function, interrelate, and serve as a means for identifying potential risk	
d.	This type of diagram method includes graphical representations of situations that show causal influences, time ordering of events, and other types of relationships between variables and potential outcomes.	

18.	**This method is used to identify potential risks before your project has even begun. You will review your project and compare it with past projects. Determine what could go right or wrong by combing through the past evidence using key sources of information, like historical records. Name the method.**	
a.	Pre-Mortem Analysis	
b.	A Failure Modes and Effect Analysis	

c.	A SWOT Analysis	
d.	Root Cause Identification	

19.	**Define path convergence.**	
a.	The process of prioritizing risks for further analysis or action by assessing and combining their probability of occurrence and impact.	
b.	Multiple activities flowing into or from a central activity. To consolidate effort and remove redundancy, sometimes combining series or items is needed.	
c.	A popular, quick, and cost-effective method of prioritizing tasks. The core benefit of this is that it allows you to reduce the levels of uncertainty about your project and allows you to focus your efforts on critical areas of high priority risk.	
d.	Serves to provide core definitions for probability and impact that sit at the heart of this stage.	

20.	**Name four tools and techniques used in the Qualitative Risk Analysis process.**	
a.	Risk urgency assessment, project documents, risk score, risk categorization	
b.	Impact matrix, motivational bias, Monte Carlo, decision tree	
c.	Probability, impact, risk score, risk urgency assessment	
d.	Decision tree, cognitive bias, risk data quality assessment, impact	

21.	What is a probability and impact matrix?	
a.	It shows the risk ratings and overall priority of all risks. These can be as simple as you like or as complex as required depending on the method you choose.	
b.	They determine how detailed each risk response should be. High risk scores mean high levels of response; low risk scores mean low levels of response.	
c.	It refers to the consequences that the risk will have on the project should the event ever happen.	
d.	It is an assigned score called a Risk Rating. If they are too high, you will have to find a way to remove the cause of that risk.	

22.	Name the two most important outputs in qualitative risk analysis.	
a.	The Risk Register and Trends List	
b.	The Category Groups and Impact Matrix	
c.	The Urgent List and Watch List	
d.	Positive and Negative Risk	

23.	How do you calculate risk exposure?	
a.	Category Grouping > Risk Score > Risk Analysis > Risk Exposure	
b.	Risk Rating > Risk Analysis > Risk Score > Project Risk Score > Risk Exposure	
c.	Probability > Impact > Risk Score > Project Risk Score > Risk Exposure	

d.	Risk Score > Risk Rating > Risk Exposure Calculation	

24.	**What is meant by probability and impact scoring?**	
a.	This is a highly critical process in qualitative risk analysis. It needs to be approved by all stakeholders and included in your Organizational Process Assets as a type of Probability and Impact Matrix.	
b.	Finding unbiased sources to help score risks will make them as accurate as possible. Qualitative Risk Analysis needs accurate and unbiased data if it is going to be applicable in your strategy.	
c.	Your urgency levels need to be defined, documented, and confirmed by your team and stakeholders. Build a probability and impact matrix that will allow prioritization based on score.	
d.	If you are scoring probability between 1 and 5 on a scale, then you need to detail what kind of factors would make up a score of 4. This will help remove bias and will improve how you analyze quantity.	

25.	**Which statement is the most accurate?**	
a.	In context, all quantitative analysis should undergo many rounds of analysis by anyone who is interested in improving the process. Old beliefs in feedback analysis only pertaining to qualitative data need to be reformed.	

b.	In context, all qualitative analysis should be exposed to many rounds of analysis by anyone who is interested in improving the process. Old beliefs in secondary analysis only pertaining to quantitative data need to be reformed.	
c.	In context, all probability analysis should be exposed to many rounds of risk by anyone who is interested in improving the process. Old beliefs in impact analysis only pertaining to quantitative data need to be reformed.	
d.	In context, all risk analysis should be exposed to many rounds of testing by anyone who is interested in improving the process. Old beliefs in management only pertaining to contextual data need to be reformed.	

Answer Key:

1:C	2:D	3:B	4:D	5:D	6:B	7:B	8:D	9:A	10:D
11:D	12:A	13:B	14:B	15:A	16:C	17:D	18:A	19:B	20:C
21:A	22:C	23:C	24:A	25:B					

Result:

1–10 Correct

You need to review all work up to qualitative risk analysis again to become more familiar with the concepts and calculations.

10–15 Correct

You know an average amount about the content, but perhaps another review would benefit you when you take the test.

15–20 Correct

You know most of the work—great! But the PMI questions will be challenging, so it is best to review key concepts again.

All 25 Correct

Excellent! You rose to the challenge and received a perfect score—well done!

REFERENCES

Chapter 1:

Risk Management Quotes, http://riskarticles.com/wp-content/uploads/2013/12/Risk-Management-Quotes-eBook.pdf

Egeland, Brad, *Earning Respect as a Project Manager by Delivering Consistently,* http://blog.entry.com/earn-project-management-respect

Feldman, Jonathan, *Project Management Is Finally Getting Real Respect,* http://www.informationweek.com/team-building-and-staffing/project-management-is-finally-getting-real-respect/d/d-id/1093342?

Kelly, William, *Seven Ways to Build Respect as a Project Manager,* http://www.techrepublic.com/article/seven-ways-to-build-respect-as-a-project-manager/

Project Management Integrity – At Least Try to Fake It, http://www.agilistapm.com/project-management-integrity-at-least-try-to-fake-it/

Integrity in Project Management, http://kellycrew.wordpress.com/2010/10/25/integrity-in-project-management/

McGraw, Bruce, *Integrity and the Project Manager,* http://fearnoproject.com/2013/02/12/integrity-and-the-project-manager/

Ivanenko, Dmitri, Integrity in Project Management, http://blogs.pmi.org/blog/voices_on_project_management/2009/08/integrity-in-project-managemen.html'

Alkhateeb, Homam, 3 Things Tell You Why Passion Is Important for Project Managers, http://halkhateeb.wordpress.com/2013/04/17/3-things-tell-you-why-passion-is-important-for-project-managers/

Hamilton, Gary, Byatt, Gareth, Hodgkinson, Jeff, *Work Passion and Heart as Critical Behaviors: What Every Project Manager Should Bear in Mind,* https://pmicie.org/images/downloads/Articles/9_general_article_work_passion_final.pdf

Igniting the Passion – What Motivates Project, http://pmperspectives.org/article.php?view=full&aid=58

Bourne, Lynda, *Leadership: The Mission Is Vision,* http://blogs.pmi.org/blog/voices_on_project_management/2013/04/leadership-the-mission-is-visi.html

Kavanagh, John, *Project Managers Must Share Their Vision To Ensure Success,* http://www.computerweekly.com/feature/Project-managers-must-share-their-vision-to-ensure-success

Egeland, Brad, *Project Management: Having Vision,* http://pmtips.net/project-management-vision/

Fitzgerald, Donna, *Shares Vision: A Key to Project Success,* http://www.techrepublic.com/article/shared-vision-a-key-to-project-success/

Chapter 2:

Risk Management Quotes, http://riskarticles.com/wp-content/uploads/2013/12/Risk-Management-Quotes-eBook.pdf

PMI Risk Management Professional (PMI-RMP®), http://www.pmi.org/Certification/PMI-Risk-Management-Professional-PMI-RMP.aspx

PMI-RMP® Exam Guidance, http://www.pmi.org/en/Certification/PMI-Risk-Management-Professional-PMI-RMP/PMI-RMP-Exam-Prep.aspx

PMI Risk Management Professional (PMI – RMP) Exam Content Outline, http://www.pmi.org/~/media/Files/PDF/Certification/PMI-RMP%20Exam%20Content%20Outline_Final.ashx

PMI Risk Management Professional (PMI-RMP®) Handbook, http://www.pmi.org/Certification/~/media/PDF/Certifications/pmi-RMP_handbook.ashx

Chapter 3:

Risk Management Quotes, http://riskarticles.com/wp-content/uploads/2013/12/Risk-Management-Quotes-eBook.pdf

What Is Project Management? http://www.pmi.org/About-Us/About-Us-What-is-Project-Management.aspx

What Is Project Management? http://www.apm.org.uk/WhatIsPM

5 Basic Phases Of Project Management, http://www.projectinsight.net/project-management-basics/basic-project-management-phases

What Is Project Management? http://www.mpug.com/education/what-is-project-management/

Purdy, Kevin, *What the Hell Is Project Management, Anyway?* http://www.fastcompany.com/1822525/what-hell-project-management-anyway

Investopedia Explains 'Project Management,' http://www.investopedia.com/terms/p/project-management.asp

Chapter 4:

101 Quotations for Project Managers, http://management.simplicable.com/management/new/101-quotations-for-project-managers

Risk Management Plan, https://www.phe.gov/about/amcg/toolkit/Documents/risk-management.pdf

Plan Risk Management Process, http://www.pm-primer.com/plan-risk-management/

11.2 Risk Management Process, http://pm4id.org/11/2/

Project Management/PMBOK/Risk Management, http://en.wikibooks.org/wiki/Project_Management/PMBOK/Risk_Management#Inputs

Risk Management Planning, http://www.anticlue.net/archives/000812.htm

Risk Management – Useful Tools and Techniques, https://success. clarizen.com/entries/24127786-Risk-Management-Useful-Tools-and-Techniques

Duff, Victoria, *Risk Management Tools and Techniques,* http://smallbusiness.chron.com/risk-management-tools-techniques-4569. html

Chapter 5:

Risk Management Quotes, http://riskviews.wordpress.com/risk-management-quotes/

Hillson, David, *Using Risk Metalanguage to Develop Risk Responses,* http://www.risk-doctor.com/pdf-briefings/risk-doctor22e.pdf

Risk Register, http://en.wikipedia.org/wiki/Risk_register

Hulett, David, *Risk Register Development,* http://www.projectrisk. com/risk_register_development.html

Enterprise Risk Management Tools and Techniques for Effective Implementation, http://erm.ncsu.edu/az/erm/i/chan/m-articles/documents/IMAToolsTechniquesMay07.pdf

Tools and Techniques to Identify Project Risks, http://stolenlantern. blogspot.com/2013/02/tools-and-techniques-to-identify.html

Risk Identification Methods – 12 Types, https://manager.clearrisk.com/ Resources/RiskTool/Risk_Identification_Methods_-_12_Types

Managing Risks: A New Framework, http://hbr.org/2012/06/ managing-risks-a-new-framework/ar/1

Risk Identification Examples, http://oag.treasury.gov.za/RMF/ RMF%20Documents/Examples/07.%20Example%20Risk%20 Identification.pdf

Example of a Documented Risk Management Process, http://www.deir.qld.gov.au/workplace/resources/pdfs/ divingriskman_02example2005.pdf

Risk Identification, http://www.mypmps.net/en/mypmps/ knowledgeareas/risk/risk-identification.html

Project Management: Identifying Risk in Your Project, http://certifedpmp.

wordpress.com/2008/10/13/identifying-risks-in-your-project/

Rajman, Rawi, *Project Risk Identification for New Project Manager,* http://www.projecttimes.com/articles/project-risk-identification-for-new-project-manager.html

Chapter 6:

McDonald, Mildred Lynn, *25 Invigorating Project Management Quotes,* http://svprojectmanagement.com/25-invigorating-project-management-quotes

Qualitative Risk Analysis, http://www.mypmps.net/en/mypmps/knowledgeareas/risk/qualitative-risk-analysis.html

Risk Urgency Assessment, http://getpmpcertified.blogspot.com/2013/01/risk-urgency-assessment.html

Qualitative Risk Analysis, http://www.businessdictionary.com/definition/qualitative-risk-analysis.html

Qualitative Risk Analysis, http://www.mypmps.net/en/mypmps/knowledgeareas/risk/qualitative-risk-analysis.html

Project Management Knowledge: Path Convergence, http://project-management-knowledge.com/definitions/p/path-convergence/

Perform Qualitative Risk Analysis, http://www.pm-primer.com/perform-qualitative-risk-analysis/

Perform Qualitative Risk Analysis, http://www.testeagle.com/classroom/sample-lesson-perform-qualitative-risk-analysis.aspx

Perform Qualitative Risk Analysis, http://anamulhuq.blogspot.com/2012/01/risk-managment-113-perform-qualitative.html

Rowley, Jerome, *5th Edition PMBOK® Guide – Chapter 11: Process 11.3 – Perform Qualitative Risk Analysis,* http://4squareviews.com/2013/08/01/5th-edition-pmbok-guide-chapter-11-process-11-3-perform-qualitative-risk-analysis/

Chapter 7:

Risk Management Quotes, http://riskviews.wordpress.com/risk-management-quotes/

Leadership Laboratory: Qualitative VS Qualitative Risk Assessment, http://www.sans.edu/research/leadership-laboratory/article/risk-assessment

Qualitative Risk Analysis and Assessment, http://www.project-management-skills.com/qualitative-risk-analysis.html

Mochal, Tom, *Use These Steps on Qualitative Analysis of Project Risks,* http://www.techrepublic.com/article/use-these-steps-in-qualitative-analysis-of-project-risks/

PMP® Exam Tip: Why Do We Use a Probability and Impact Matrix, https://www.project-management-prepcast.com/index.php/freetry-it/free-pmp-tips/pmp-exam-tips/315-pmp-exam-tip-why-do-we-use-a-probability-and-impact-matrix

Risk Impact/Probability Chart, Learning To Prioritize Risks, http://www.mindtools.com/pages/article/newPPM_78.htm*Risk Scoring Method Description,* http://docs.oracle.com/cd/E17266_01/p6help/help/en/helpmain.htm?toc.htm?44763.htm

Van der Berg, Harry, *Reanalyzing Qualitative Interviews From Different Angles: The Risk of Decontextualization and Other Problems of Sharing Qualitative Data,* http://www.qualitative-research.net/index.php/fqs/article/view/499/1074

Chapter 8:

Quantitative Quotes, http://www.brainyquote.com/quotes/keywords/quantitative.html

Quantitative Risk Analysis. http://www.mypmps.net/en/mypmps/knowledgeareas/risk/quantitative-risk-analysis.html

Tedero, *PMBOK Chapter 11- Project Risk Management,* http://www.cram.com/flashcards/pmbok-chapter-11-project-risk-management-1873570

Kumar, Anand, Vijaya, *Continuous Distributions,* http://getpmpcertified.blogspot.com/2013/02/continuous-distributions.html

Kohrell, Dave, *PERT Formula – 5th Edition PMBOK,* http://tapuniversity.com/2013/10/19/pert-formula/

PERT Three Point Estimation Technique, http://www.pmdocuments. com/2012/09/17/pert-three-point-estimation-technique/

PMP Study – Part 23 – Performing Risk Analysis, Flashcards, http:// quizlet.com/21173534/pmp-study-part-23-performing-risk-analysis-flash-cards/

Risk Analysis, http://www.palisade.com/risk/risk_analysis.asp

Rowley, Jerome, *5th Edition PMBOK® Guide-Data Gathering Representation Techniques For Risk Management,* http://4squareviews. com/2013/08/05/5th-edition-pmbok-guide-data-gathering-and-representation-techniques-for-risk-management/

Marom, Shim, *Project Risk Management and the Application of Monte Carlo Simulation,* http://quantmleap.com/blog/2010/07/project-risk-management-and-the-application-of-monte-carlo-simulation/

Chapter 9:

Some Favourite Quotes on Risk Management, http://31000risk. blogspot.com/2011/04/some-favourite-quotes-on-risk.html

Wicklin, Rick, *That Distribution Is Quite PERT,* http://blogs.sas.com/ content/iml/2012/10/24/pert-distribution/

Chapter 54: Performing Quantitative Analysis, http://getpmpcertified. blogspot.com/2011_06_01_archive.html

Chandler, David, L, *Explained: Sigma – How Do You Know When a New Finding Is Significant? The Sigma Value Can Tell You – But Watch Out for Dead Fish,* http://newsoffice.mit.edu/2012/explained-sigma-0209

Tornado Diagram, http://en.wikipedia.org/wiki/Tornado_diagram

PERT Three Point Estimation Technique, http://www.pmdocuments. com/2012/09/17/pert-three-point-estimation-technique/

PMP Study – Part 23 – Performing Risk Analysis, http://quizlet. com/21173534/pmp-study-part-23-performing-risk-analysis-flash-cards/

Marom, Shim, *Project Risk Management and the Application of Monte Carlo Simulation,* http://quantmleap.com/blog/2010/07/project-risk-management-and-the-application-of-monte-carlo-simulation/

Chapter 11:

Risk Quotes, http://thinkexist.com/quotations/risk/2.html

PMBOK Control Risks, http://www.pm-primer.com/control-risks/

Rowley, Jerome, *5ᵗʰ Edition PMBOK® Guide – Chapter 4: Change Management Plan,* http://4squareviews.com/2013/02/28/5th-edition-pmbok-guide-chapter-4-change-management-plan/

Chapter 12:

Best Risk Management Quotes, http://riskviews.wordpress.com/2010/01/12/best-risk-management-quotes/

Governance in the Boardroom: How Project Management Can Deliver Organizational Strategy, https://iccpm.com/sites/default/files/kcfinder/files/YButler%20The_Role_of_Project_Management_and_Governance_in_Strategy_Implementation%20160808.pdf

Chapter 13:

Stakeholder Power/Interest Analysis, http://requirementstechniques. wordpress.com/stakeholder-analysis/stakeholder-powerinterest-analysis/

Famous Advice on Decision-Making, Uncertainty and Risk Management, http://www.adviceonmanagement.com/advice_uncertainty.html

PMP Series: Project Communication Management, http://resources.intenseschool.com/pmp-series-project-communication-management/

Yeomans, Daniel C., *Passing the Risk Management Certification the First Time!* Dog Ear Publishing, United State of America.

INDEX

A

AC (Actual Costs) 191, 193, 197
Achievement motivation theory 208, 209
Activity cost estimates 49, 72, 73, 82
Additional analysis 104, 105, 114
Affinity diagramming 78
Analyzing risk process performance against established metrics 32
Assessment of stakeholder risk 30
Assumptions analysis 49, 72, 76, 83

B

BAC (Budget At Completion) 191, 192, 193
Being accountable 12
Beta distributions 124, 126, 140
Bias 97, 109, 150
Brainstorming sessions 18
Budget constraints 63
Buffer analysis 205, 206
Building innovation 17
Building risk management plans 44, 222, 223

C

Calculating communication channels 213, 214
Category grouping 104, 105, 114, 230
Cause and effect diagrams 76
Change requests 50
Checklist analysis 49, 72, 76, 83
Coaching directive 212
Communicating risks to your stakeholders and team members 44
Communications Management Plan 213, 214
Competent decision maker 19
Competent project management system 17

S

ABOUT THE AUTHOR

Hasnain Rizvi is a PMI OPM3® Certified Consultant with formal project, program, portfolio management, and governance experience. He has performed project management maturity assessment work and managed mission critical complex programs and projects for Global 2000 and Fortune 500 clients.

Hasnain is currently the CIO, Principal Agile Coach & Director of Education at AAA Institute, as well as Founder of GlocalPM, Inc. He has performed project management maturity assessment work and supported clients in establishing and redesigning project management offices (PMOs) across various sectors. He has managed complex programs in IBM's Project Management practice in Saskatchewan, Canada. He has provided extensive project management services to The Government of Newfoundland and Labrador. Hasnain's specialties include planning and implementing mitigation activities to assist in recovering troubled projects.

Hasnain is pursuing his research interests in agile methodologies and coaching through graduate work at SKEMA Business School in France. He is a graduate of Caltech's Project Management Program.

Hasnain has trained and mentored over 15,000 professionals across the globe. He is an adjunct instructor with several universities and colleges, including The University of British Columbia and SAIT Polytechnic. He is an acclaimed professional speaker and trainer. Hasnain currently provides the following certification track coaching: PMP, CBAP, PMI-ACP, PMI-RMP, PMI-SP, CISM, Lean Six Sigma and ITIL Foundations.